Other Books by the Same Author

So I Can Laugh Again
I Shall See Evil No More
I Am Committed to You
For further inquiries, send your email to bojolomi@yahoo.com

THE POWER BEHIND A BLESSED LIFE

UNDERSTANDING THE SECRET OF ABRAHAM'S BLESSING

Benson Olomuro Oritsejolomisan

WESTBOW
PRESS®
A DIVISION OF THOMAS NELSON
& ZONDERVAN

This book is a work of non-fiction. Unless otherwise noted, and in some cases, names of people and places have been altered to protect their privacy.

WestBow Press books may be ordered through booksellers or by contacting:

WestBow Press
A Division of Thomas Nelson & Zondervan
1663 Liberty Drive
Bloomington, IN 47403
www.westbowpress.com
1 (866) 928-1240

Because of the dynamic nature of the Internet, any web addresses or links contained in this book may have changed since publication and may no longer be valid. The views expressed in this work are solely those of the author and do not necessarily reflect the views of the publisher, and the publisher hereby disclaims any responsibility for them.

Any people depicted in stock imagery provided by Thinkstock are models, and such images are being used for illustrative purposes only. Certain stock imagery © Thinkstock.

ISBN: 978-1-9736-1596-5 (sc)
ISBN: 978-1-9736-1597-2 (hc)
ISBN: 978-1-9736-1595-8 (e)

Library of Congress Control Number: 2018900822

Print information available on the last page.

WestBow Press rev. date: 08/02/2018

CONTENTS

DEDICATION

This book is dedicated first to my Father God, who, out of His love, showed me mercy by bringing me into the covenant of the blessing. It is also dedicated to everyone in the body of Christ who believes that *the blessing of the Lord makes one rich.*

ACKNOWLEDGMENTS

I am thankful to Dr. Sam and Dr. (Mrs.) Love Amaga, my parents and mentors in the Lord. Your love, patience, and leadership skills have brought me to where I am today. The Holy Spirit will continually rest His hand on you. I am forever grateful.

I am deeply grateful to the team of committed believers who made this work possible. To the editorial team, Mrs. Nkemamaka Okoroafor Esq, Barr. (Mrs.) Bukola Anuwe, and Evangelist Jane Ofunne–Ihejirika. I am eternally grateful. It is with particular pleasure that I express my gratitude to my colaborers, Sam Onoja, John Abang, and Elijah Obia, for their inputs.

My affectionate and deeply felt gratitude goes to my home team: my wife, Ugochi, for her love, commitment, input, and continuous support, and to my boys, Joshua, Joseph, and Josiah, for their love and understanding. You are my blessing!

INTRODUCTION

An understanding of the blessing of Abraham will make a difference in your life and cause a great turnaround for you and your family. The blessing of Abraham is a working blessing! It is the ultimate blessing. The secret of Abraham's blessing is the *foundation* upon which every blessed and successful life in the kingdom of God is built. Since its release, the blessing has been the cornerstone of God's people. From Abraham as a person to the birth of the Jewish nation, the blessing has taken care of everyone who believed in its simplicity, transforming them inside out. It took them from bondage into freedom, from the curse to the blessing, and from poverty to prosperity. The blessing of Abraham is far superior and stronger than the curse. It is still essential this day, as it was when God delivered it to Abraham, His friend. The blessing is what makes the difference between health or sickness, success or failure, wealth or poverty, strength or weakness. I strongly believe that God has brought this book your way to declare the simplicity of God's word and give hope, meaning, and joy to your life and everything that has to do with it. Get set to receive the good things of life that God has ordained for you and your loved ones via the blessing of Abraham. The blessing turned Abraham's hopeless situation around and gave him a name, greatness, and fame throughout eternity. Therefore, no matter how deprived and hopeless your case is, if you allow the blessing of Abraham into your life and walk fully with its demand, you will be amazed as your life is transformed into a blessed life. This is your moment. The blessing is alive and is working. It will manifest in multiple ways in every area of your life as it was with Abraham. It is the ultimate blessing reserved for God's chosen ones. As you lay hold of the blessing of Abraham, believe you receive it, declare that you already have it, and it shall be evident. With the blessing, you will overcome every form of lack and poverty. The Lord's blessing is yours to enjoy. In the pages that follow, you will discover as a believer in Christ Jesus that you have been destined to live a blessed life!

CHAPTER 1

THE POWER OF THE BLESSING

> I will make thee exceeding fruitful, and I will make nations of thee, and kings shall come out of thee. And I will establish my covenant between me and thee and thy seed after thee in their generations for an everlasting covenant, to be a God unto thee, and to thy seed after thee. And I will give unto thee, and to thy seed after thee, the land wherein thou art a stranger, all the land of Canaan, for an everlasting possession; and I will be their God. And God said unto Abraham, Thou shalt keep my covenant therefore, thou, and thy seed after thee in their generations. (Genesis 17:6–9)

The blessing of Abraham is designed to protect you and your loved ones from the difficult times we live in. From one country to another and on families and individuals, the heat is on. The good news is you and your family can be exempt.

As recorded in the Bible, times of difficulty and great challenge have happened several times in the past. Nothing that has happened or will happen in your life is a surprise to God, who has your best interest at heart. Before any recession, the Father already has a plan to shield you from its effect and to prosper you beyond your imagination. His plan is packaged in the blessing of Abraham.

— THE BLESSING ——————————————

> The blessing of the LORD makes one rich, and He adds
> no sorrow with it. (Proverbs 10:22 NKJV)

The blessing of the Lord is a total package and a powerful force! When it comes upon your life, it makes you an overcomer because it has the ability to affect every area of your life. As Kenneth Copeland says, "It goes all the way, from the top to the bottom and from the bottom to the top!" The blessing will make you rich in your spirit, your body, your marriage, your bank account, and everything you do.

Understand that it is not your qualification or your job that prospers you. No. A thousand times no! Your job is only a channel for the blessing to enrich your life. The scripture says, "The blessing of the LORD makes one rich." It is the responsibility of the blessing of the Lord to make you rich. Yours is to trust and believe His word.

There are multitudes of people out there who earn from five to seven figures or more monthly, yet they are miserable because the blessing of the Lord has no place to dwell in their lives. There are so many out there who make so much money yet cannot make ends meet. A college or university degree will not make you prosper! Please don't get me wrong. Education is commendable. But you must see farther than your certificate. Look around you. There are so many with multiple degrees who are broke in life. According to the word of God, it is the *blessing* that prospers you! The blessing is what makes things to produce in your life. It is the *power* behind every blessed life in God's kingdom.

In the beginning, when God created Adam and Eve, He first pronounced the blessing on them and commanded fruitfulness and multiplication upon them.

> So God created man in his own image, in the image of
> God created he him; male and female created he them.
> And God blessed them, and God said unto them, Be
> fruitful, and multiply, and replenish the earth, and

subdue it: and have dominion over the fish of the sea, and over the fowl of the air, and over every living thing that moveth upon the earth. (Genesis 1:27–28)

With the blessing pronounced by God on humans comes every intelligence and ability that is needed to subdue and have dominion over everything that was created. The blessing makes for productivity. Note that it was after God blessed them that He commanded them to be fruitful and multiply.

Whenever you allow the blessing of the Lord to operate in your life, you become so productive and fruitful that no famine or recession can affect you. The blessing of the Lord will always prevail over any situation you find yourself in.

> Lift not up your horn on high: speak not with a stiff neck. For promotion cometh neither from the east, nor from the west, nor from the south. But God is the judge: he putteth down one, and setteth up another. (Psalm 75:5–7)

The scripture above tells us God is the Judge who is responsible for the promotion or demotion of anyone. The Lord promoted Isaac, and he became the envy of the Philistines as he prevailed over famine. Others may have planted and harvested nothing or were too scared to plant. But Isaac, acting on God's instruction and knowledge (higher information), planted during the famine and received a hundredfold harvest.

> There was a famine in the land, besides the first famine that was in the days of Abraham. And Isaac went to Abimelech king of the Philistines, in Gerar. Then the Lord appeared to him and said: "Do not go down to Egypt; live in the land of which I shall tell you. Dwell in this land, and I will be with you and bless you; for to you and your descendants I give

all these lands, and I will perform the oath which I swore to Abraham your father. Then Isaac sowed in that land, and reaped in the same year a hundredfold; and the Lord blessed him. The man began to prosper, and continued prospering until he became very prosperous. (Genesis 26:1–3, 12–13 NKJV)

The blessing thus empowered him to prosper. As you begin to operate in the blessing, you will discover that the blessing is working even in famine! You cannot stop a man who is carrying the blessing of the Lord. No force on earth is able to stop you from achieving your dreams, as long as the blessing is your foundation!

— WHAT IS THE BLESSING?

The blessing is a covenant entered into by blood between God and Abraham. God initiated the process of the blessing with Abraham in a relationship before the blessing was conferred on him. After Adam betrayed God and sold out his inheritance and authority to the devil, he became a slave to Satan. God, not willing to give up, located a man named Abram and gave him a proposal.

Now the Lord had said unto Abram, Get thee out of thy country, and from thy kindred, and from thy father's house, unto a land that I will shew thee: And I will make of thee a great nation, and I will bless thee, and make thy name great; and thou shalt be a blessing: And I will bless them that bless thee, and curse him that curseth thee: and in thee shall all families of the earth be blessed. So Abram departed, as the Lord had spoken unto him; and Lot went with him: and Abram was seventy and five years old when he departed out of Haran. (Genesis 12:1–4)

It will interest you to know that the Lord did not tell Abraham where he was going. A wise person will always accept any proposal from the Lord. Abraham did. He gave his thumbs-up to go ahead with the Lord, and he was blessed beyond measure. The greatest thing in your life, after you receive Jesus Christ as your Lord and Savior, is to walk boldly into the blessing. This is possible by the revelation of the Holy Spirit. God found Abraham a suitable partner for the birthing of the gospel and conferred the blessing upon him on a platform of the covenant.

> And when Abram was ninety years old and nine, the Lord appeared to Abram, and said unto him, I am the Almighty God; walk before me, and be thou perfect. And I will make my covenant between me and thee, and will multiply thee exceedingly. And Abram fell on his face: and God talked with him, saying, As for me, behold, my covenant is with thee, and thou shalt be a father of many nations. Neither shall thy name any more be called Abram, but thy name shall be Abraham; for a father of many nations have I made thee. And I will make thee exceeding fruitful, and I will make nations of thee, and kings shall come out of thee. And I will establish my covenant between me and thee and thy seed after thee in their generations for an everlasting covenant, to be a God unto thee, and to thy seed after thee. (Genesis 17:1–7)

The blessing is a spiritual endowment with an everlasting capacity placed upon Abraham and his descendants throughout all *generations,* including yours. The blessing is active and alive today, as it was then. This is your season and time. Open up, and allow the blessing to do what God designed it for. Nothing else has the strength to transform your life like the blessing of the Lord.

– WHAT THE BLESSING DOES ─────────

The blessing makes things to supernaturally and effectively work for you. It blesses you and makes you a blessing! It is a spiritual force with the might of God that took care of Abraham in all areas of his life, with the promise of eternal redemption.

> And Abraham was old, and well stricken in age: and the Lord had blessed Abraham in all things. (Genesis 24:1)

Abraham had a relationship with God, and as long as he walked in *obedience* to God's instruction, nothing could alter the promise of God. Even when his nephew was captured by the enemy, he was not afraid to go after the four kings whose armies had come together as one and defeated five nations. As a result, they captured Lot. Empowered by the blessing of the Lord, Abraham went after the enemies.

> And it came to pass in the days of Amraphel king of Shinar, Arioch king of Ellasar, Chedorlaomer king of Elam, and Tidal king of nations; That these made war with Bera king of Sodom, and with Birsha king of Gomorrah, Shinab king of Admah, and Shemeber king of Zeboiim, and the king of Bela, which is Zoar. And there went out the king of Sodom, and the king of Gomorrah, and the king of Admah, and the king of Zeboiim, and the king of Bela (the same is Zoar;) and they joined battle with them in the vale of Siddim; With Chedorlaomer the king of Elam, and with Tidal king of nations, and Amraphel king of Shinar, and Arioch king of Ellasar; four kings with five. And the vale of Siddim was full of slimepits; and the kings of Sodom and Gomorrah fled, and fell there; and they that remained fled to the mountain. And they

took all the goods of Sodom and Gomorrah, and all their victuals, and went their way. And they took Lot, Abram's brother's son, who dwelt in Sodom, and his goods, and departed. (Genesis 14:1–2, 8–12)

Now, when Abraham heard what had happened, he armed his trained servants born in his house. These 318 men were born in Abraham's residence! He saw them grow up right under his watchful eyes and took time to invest into their lives. Abraham acted as a father before actually becoming one.

These men, along with his two friends, went after the enemies. Three hundred and twenty-one of them fought and defeated four nations, who had just vanquished the armies of five nations put together. You will recover all that the enemy has stolen from your family!

And when Abram heard that his brother was taken captive, he armed his trained servants, born in his own house, three hundred and eighteen, and pursued them unto Dan. And he divided himself against them, he and his servants, by night, and smote them, and pursued them unto Hobah, which is on the left hand of Damascus. And he brought back all the goods, and also brought again his brother Lot, and his goods, and the women also, and the people. (Genesis 14:14–16)

When the blessing is at work in your life, the opposition may be more in everything, in terms of numbers, weaponry, wealth, and the rest, but they are bound to be crushed. Read through the Bible and you will see men and women, boys and girls, who brought great powers and great nations to their feet, because they walked in the blessing of Abraham. Never underestimate the power of God's ultimate blessing working in your life!

It was the blessing that empowered David over Goliath, Gideon and his men over the Midianites, and the nation of Judah over three nations: Moab, Ammon, and Mount Seir.

— THE BLESSING IS TRANSFERABLE —

The blessing of the Lord did not stop with Abraham. When God enacted the covenant of the blessing with Abraham, He made it very clear that it is an everlasting agreement between Him and Abraham and all his descendants throughout all generation.

— ISAAC —

When God pronounced the blessing upon Abraham, He promised to establish His covenant with Isaac.

> My covenant will I establish with Isaac, which Sarah shall bear unto thee at this set time in the next year. (Genesis 17:21 NKJV)

That was exactly what He did. When God says a thing, it must come to pass: every promise of God in the scripture is dependable!

Isaac faced his own challenges in life. When there was a great famine in the land, he thought of running away to Egypt but operated in the blessing and turned his whole life around to the extent that he was mightier than a whole nation.

> And there was a famine in the land, beside the first famine that was in the days of Abraham. And Isaac went unto Abimelech king of the Philistines unto Gerar. And the Lord appeared unto him, and said, Go not down into Egypt; dwell in the land which I shall tell thee of: Sojourn in this land, and I will be with thee, and will bless thee; for unto thee, and unto thy seed, I will give all these countries, and I will perform

the oath which I sware unto Abraham thy father; And
I will make thy seed to multiply as the stars of heaven,
and will give unto thy seed all these countries; and in
thy seed shall all the nations of the earth be blessed;
Because that Abraham obeyed my voice, and kept
my charge, my commandments, my statutes, and my
laws. And Isaac dwelt in Gerar. (Genesis 26:1–6)

Isaac was blessed because he was a descendant of Abraham.
Similarly, all who belong to Jesus Christ are descendants of Abraham
by faith and are thus entitled to God's blessings conferred on Abraham
(Galatians 3:28–29 NCV). Where others failed, he excelled. My father
in the Lord will always say "my case is different" Isaac's case was
different, because he carried the blessing of Abraham.

And the man waxed great, and went forward, and
grew until he became very great: For he had possession
of flocks, and possession of herds, and great store
of servants: and the Philistines envied him. And
Abimelech said unto Isaac, Go from us; for thou art
much mightier than we. (Genesis 26:13–14, 16)

Even in the midst of threats, the Lord was with him every step
of the way, reminding him of the blessing of his father Abraham.
The Lord appeared to him the same night and said, "I am the God
of Abraham your father. Fear not, for I am with you and will favor
you with blessings and multiply your descendants for the sake of
My servant Abraham" (Genesis 26:24 AMPC). The blessing of the
Lord transformed the life of Isaac greatly. He was so blessed that the
Philistines envied him. The blessing made him mighty! One man
became a threat to a whole nation. The king said to him, "Go from
us; for thou art much mightier than we." The blessing operates in
every generation. As long as you allow the blessing to work in your
life, it will turn things around. Indeed, the blessing of Abraham is
the power that makes one a blessed person.

— JACOB

Next in line was the man named Jacob, the son of Isaac. When Jacob was leaving his father's house, he virtually left with nothing, except a walking stick. He was down to ground zero with no spare clothing and had to use a stone for a pillow. But he had something far greater than any material possession; he had the blessing of the Lord on him. God has never failed anyone who believes in the blessing of Abraham.

Jacob started his life as an employee of Laban. For years, Laban, who became his father-in-law, cheated him ten times, but that could not stop the blessing from working as he became more prosperous than his employer. Nothing is strong or big enough to short circuit the blessing from working. The blessing made a way where there seemed to be no way. We are told in scriptures, "Thus the man became exceedingly prosperous, and had large flocks, female and male servants, and camels and donkeys" (Genesis 30:43). Remember, he left his father's house with only a walking stick. But he returned in droves! No matter your situation, the blessing will turn it around and make you a working blessing!

— JOSEPH

Now we come to this lovely man named Joseph. As a seed of Abraham who obeyed God, the blessing could not be stopped in his life. When his ten brothers wanted to kill him, the blessing intervened and they changed their mind and threw him into a pit instead. Even as a slave, the blessing prospered him, and his master noticed it. In the prison, it was the blessing that prospered him. Finally, the blessing gave him one big giant leap—from the prison to the palace, as the prime minister!

> Thou shalt be over my house, and according unto thy
> word shall all my people be ruled: only in the throne

will I be greater than thou. And Pharaoh said unto Joseph, See, I have set thee over all the land of Egypt. And Pharaoh took off his ring from his hand, and put it upon Joseph's hand, and arrayed him in vestures of fine linen, and put a gold chain about his neck; And he made him to ride in the second chariot which he had; and they cried before him, Bow the knee: and he made him ruler over all the land of Egypt. (Genesis 41:40–43)

From becoming a slave boy to a prisoner and later the prime minister of the greatest nation on earth as at that time, Joseph excelled on the weight of the blessing of Abraham. There was no luck or coincidence with Joseph as it was the power of the blessing that set him up to reign in Egypt.

The greatest deal you can ever have in life is to walk right into the blessing of Abraham. Read through the Bible, and you will notice that from one generation to another everyone who stood out with God had a transformed destiny. Remember, it is the blessing that makes you rich. I believe that you are next in line for the blessing to prosper!

CHAPTER 2

THE ASSURANCE OF THE BLESSING

> Wherein God, willing more abundantly to shew unto the heirs of promise the immutability of his counsel, confirmed it by an oath: That by two immutable things, in which it was impossible for God to lie, we might have a strong consolation, who have fled for refuge to lay hold upon the hope set before us. (Hebrews 6:17–18)

Why did Abraham have so much confidence in the blessing? Abraham knew a secret about God—a secret that you and I need to know and embrace. Knowing the secret of Abraham will change your perspective about the promises of God. He demonstrated such a rare and courageous faith to the extent that he was ready to sacrifice his only son, the heir apparent whom he loved so much and who was supposed to carry on the inheritance.

> And Isaac spake unto Abraham his father, and said, My father: and he said, Here am I, my son. And he said, Behold the fire and the wood: but where is the lamb for a burnt offering? And Abraham said, My son, God will provide himself a lamb for a burnt offering: so they went both of them together. And they came to the place which God had told him of; and Abraham

built an altar there, and laid the wood in order, and
bound Isaac his son, and laid him on the altar upon
the wood. And Abraham stretched forth his hand,
and took the knife to slay his son. (Genesis 22:6–10)

You will notice that Abraham spoke to his son with such certainty
of God's provision of a lamb. Why? Abraham knew the nature of
God, that the almighty God is holy! This knowledge of the holiness
of God is what gives assurance to the blessing of Abraham. The
nature of God is the backbone of Abraham's blessing. The assurance
of Abraham's blessing is resident in the very nature of the almighty
God. The God and Father of our Lord Jesus Christ is altogether holy.
The holiness of God is what sets Him apart as the almighty Creator,
who created all things. As long as God is holy, you can depend on the
blessing of Abraham. There is no other god who is holy besides the
Lord our God. The Almighty alone is holy.

And the four beasts had each of them six wings about
him; and they were full of eyes within: and they rest
not day and night, saying, Holy, holy, holy, Lord
God Almighty, which was, and is, and is to come.
(Revelation 4:8)

These four beasts that are around about the throne of the Almighty
rest not, night or day. Their duty is to worship God twenty-four hours
every day, saying nothing other than "Holy, holy, holy, Lord God
Almighty ..." Holiness and righteousness are the foundation of His
throne. Everything He does comes out of His holiness and love, and
as a result, He cannot tell a lie. He is not afraid of anyone, and neither
is He seeking the favor of any. His word is true in all circumstances.

In hope of eternal life which God, who cannot lie,
promised before time began. (Titus 1:2)

A person may tell a lie when he is afraid of someone or something or when he is seeking for a favor and for many other reasons. A person can tell a lie, but not God. Scriptures upon scriptures state the fact that the God of Abraham, Isaac, and Jacob *cannot lie.*

> For men verily swear by the greater: and an oath for confirmation is to them an end of all strife. Wherein God, willing more abundantly to shew unto the heirs of promise the immutability of his counsel, confirmed it by an oath: That by two immutable things, in which it was impossible for God to lie, we might have a strong consolation, who have fled for refuge to lay hold upon the hope set before us. (Hebrews 6:16–18)

By His unalterable and unchangeable manner, it is impossible for the God of the blessing of Abraham to lie. He said these things, so you do not have to give in to fear or doubt. God has bound or committed Himself to His word. In the book of Psalms, the Lord reassured King David of His commitment to bring to pass everything He told the king of Israel. God said to him, "My covenant I will not break, Nor alter the word that has gone out of My lips. Once I have sworn by My holiness; I will not lie to David" (Psalm 89:34–35 NKJV). To assure David of His continued desire to bless him and his offspring, God swore by His holiness. What He says to one, He says to all. The Lord has also sworn never to lie to you. God's greatest reputation is His holiness. His nature of holiness is as good as God Himself. To let you rest assured, He swore by His holiness.

When the prophet Isaiah saw the Lord's glory in His holiness, he concluded he was a dead man. Why? His holiness is breathtaking, heart-stopping, and incredibly amazing.

> It was in the year King Uzziah died that I saw the Lord. He was sitting on a lofty throne, and the train of his robe filled the Temple. Attending him were mighty seraphim, each having six wings. With two wings they covered their faces, with two they covered

their feet, and with two they flew. They were calling out to each other, "Holy, holy, holy is the Lord of Heaven's Armies! The whole earth is filled with his glory!"(Isaiah 6:1–3 NLT)

All that these powerful seraphim can say as they cry one to another is, "Holy, holy, holy, is the Lord of hosts." The Lord's glory comes from His holiness, shining forth and filling the whole earth. God's holiness is the backbone of the blessing of Abraham. The strength behind the Lord's blessing is *holiness*. Be assured the blessing is dependable.

Take away God's holiness and the Lord's blessing will be nothing, and God Himself nothing. But God be praised, He cannot be separated from His holiness. The scripture says that even when we deny Him, He cannot deny Himself. He is holy; holiness is the very nature of God. It is the very breath of God. God's holiness, His throne, and the Lord of host Himself are behind the blessing of Abraham. Due to His holiness, He cannot change His promises. We are told in scripture that God is the same all the time, yesterday, today, and forever. He remains the same.

This is our confidence that God is *holy*, and therefore, He cannot let down anyone. He did not disappoint David the shepherd boy; neither will He disappoint you, as long as you dare to trust Him.

> God is not a man, that he should lie; neither the son of man, that he should repent: hath he said, and shall he not do it? Or hath he spoken, and shall he not make it good? (Numbers 23:19)

Everything God promised, He will make good in your life. He is true to every one of His promises.

For you to know the backbone of the blessing of Abraham, The Lord said, "If ye can break my covenant of the day, and my covenant of the night, and that there should not be day and night in their season; Then may also my covenant be broken with David my servant, that he should not have a son to reign upon his throne; and with the Levites the priests, my ministers" (Jeremiah 33:20–21). Every day that you wake up in the morning and go to bed at night is evidence that God's blessing reigns supreme. Understanding the nature of God, that as a result of His holiness and love, He cannot lie, will boost your faith. Read through the Bible and feed on His holiness and see your faith take a giant stride.

Everything the Lord does is as a result of His holiness and love for humanity. This is the foundation for prosperity in the kingdom. You must rest in the truth that God is holy, and He loves you personally. He wants you blessed to the extent that you will become a blessing. God is too holy and righteous to fail!

CHAPTER 3

IS THE CURSE STRONGER?

God said unto Balaam, Thou shalt not go with them;
thou shalt not curse the people: for they are blessed.
(Numbers 22:12)

Is the curse stronger than the blessing? No. A million times no!
The blessing is always stronger than the curse. Are you enjoying
the blessing of the Lord or struggling from one disappointment to
another? As a believer in Christ Jesus, you are designed to walk in
the blessing of the Lord. Unfortunately, so many are under the yoke
of the taskmaster.

— TWO FORCES AT WORK

Have you taken an inventory of your life and family recently?
Is there a history of constant disappointment, frustrations, and
tragedies that seem to be endless and beyond explanation? In both
cases, an invisible force is at work. There are two forces at work in
the earth. They are:

- the force of the blessing, and
- the force of the curse.

The force at work in you determines your destiny for good or for
bad. Watching others with less qualifications and less motivation

achieve the results that have eluded you brings you dissatisfaction and frustration. You just know that you are struggling against something you cannot identify.

Remember, the force at work in you determines the outcome of your destiny, for good or for bad. The pattern may not be the same, but you can see the same trend affecting your family, health, business, career, or finances. Do you want to stop the cycle of failure, misfortune and constant disappointment in your life and family? That is what this book is out to address. There is a need to allow the blessing access into your spirit. Let the blessing live in your spirit because what controls or influences your spirit directs the outcome of your life and destiny. You need to take note of the fact that your spirit is the engine room of your life.

There are two opposing forces operating on the earth; these forces do not operate according to natural laws. The force you allow to work for you will determine your destiny. The force of the blessing will produce good, while the force of the curse will produce evil. The will of God for your life is to embrace the force of the blessing. For any child of God who believes in Jesus Christ, your account has already been credited with the force of the blessing.

— TYPES OF CURSES

There are various kinds of curses:

- the curse of man
- the self-inflicted curse
- the curse of the devil
- the curse of God

There are principles guiding the operation of the blessing and the curse. These principles do not respect status or color. Once you come under its jurisdiction, the effect begins to produce, and no kind of curse has the right to come upon you without your permission, directly or indirectly.

— THE CURSE OF MAN

This form of curse is so powerful and has been responsible for the undoing of so many destinies. Speaking negative words on your offspring is as bad as pronouncing the curse on them. Be careful not to use negative words on your children. In the realm of the spirit, words matter a lot, and nothing is taken for granted.

NOAH

The first case of a father speaking negative words over his offspring is Noah as recorded in the book of Genesis. After the flood, Noah cultivated the land and planted a vineyard.

> And he drank of the wine, and was drunken; and he was uncovered within his tent. And Ham, the father of Canaan, saw the nakedness of his father, and told his two brethren without. (Genesis 9:21–22)

Ham made a mockery of his father by speaking of the father's nakedness to his brothers. When Noah recovered from his drunkenness and knew what Ham had done, he was upset and angry. "And he said, Cursed be Canaan; *a servant of servants shall he be* unto his brethren" (Genesis 9:25, emphasis mine). He was so dissatisfied with his son's action that he said three times that Ham will be a slave to his brothers (Genesis 9:25–27). According to that proclamation of Noah, Canaan became a servant for many generations. Please be careful.

JACOB

In the life of Jacob, we see how his word affected the destinies of his children. Jacob had twelve sons, and among them were three who lacked restraint and were agents of cruelty and heartache to their father, Reuben, Simeon, and Levi.

> Reuben, thou art my firstborn, my might, and the beginning of my strength, the excellency of dignity, and the excellency of power: Unstable as water, thou shalt not excel; because thou wentest up to thy father's bed; then defiledst thou it: he went up to my couch. Simeon and Levi are brethren; instruments of cruelty are in their habitations. O my soul, come not thou into their secret; unto their assembly, mine honour, be not thou united: for in their anger they slew a man, and in their selfwill they digged down a wall. Cursed be their anger, for it was fierce; and their wrath, for it was cruel: I will divide them in Jacob, and scatter them in Israel. (Genesis 49:3–7)

These three sons had such bright and glorious futures by virtue of the covenant of the blessing of Abraham, but by foolishness as demonstrated by their actions, they missed the inheritance and embraced the curse. As children or people under authority, we must be very careful that our actions do not bring shame and disgrace to our parents or the one whose authority we are under.

Furthermore, we see another kind of the curse of man in place when a fellow man or woman is upset and angry with a person and as a result opens his or her mouth to rain down evil words upon that person. If that person is at fault, the curses will take effect. But if that person is innocent, forget it; the person cursing is wasting his time. No curse will be upon that person. "Curses will not harm someone who is innocent; they are like sparrows or swallows that fly around and never land" (Proverbs 26:2 NCV). The word *innocent* above has nothing to do with your actions or good deeds as a person. Rather, it is because in Christ Jesus we have been absolved of all guilt and declared innocent. But to him who has no covering in Christ Jesus, as long as the curse is coming from a high-powered vessel, it will land on the target and cause havoc. Outside Christ Jesus the human race has become evil inclined.

A wicked person will take offense at his or her neighbor and pronounce evil words for no just reason. King David knew this, so he prayed to God to show respect for the covenant. Why? Cruelty has become a common occurrence on the face of the earth due to the evil work of darkness (Psalm 74:24). On this earth, our only place of refuge and safety is Jesus Christ. For in Him "the curse causeless shall not come" (Proverbs 26:2).

— THE SELF-INFLICTED CURSE

As the name implies, this kind of curse is not pronounced by anyone but oneself. So many are suffering under self-inflicted curses. By saying and doing things that are against progress, people are inflicting curses on themselves.

Some years back, a young lady appeared in a church office crying and pleading to see my father in the Lord, Dr. Sam Amaga. She had rashes all over her and was burning and itching restlessly. When my father heard her cry, he asked that she be brought in to see him. Her story was that the rashes and itching had defied all forms of medical treatment, which made her resort to spiritual help, and in the process, she was taken to a man of God in another state for deliverance and prayer. As the man of God stretched out his hand to pray, he withdrew his hand and told her that she had spoken against a man of God and needed to go and apologize because his prayer would not help her. She narrated how she was in the company of the scornful and had joined to castigate my father in the Lord. My father just laughed at her and told her she was forgiven. He said, "Be healed," and that was the end of her affliction. Whatever a person condemns and hates will be far from such a person. Have you been speaking against wealth and prosperity? I used to know a "Christian" lady who had nothing good to say about preachers who taught on prosperity. She castigated and condemned these men of God because they believe and preach that believers ought to prosper according to scripture. Some years later, she called me on the phone sounding miserable and in financial distress, asking me to help her with a job. You cannot condemn a thing and enjoy its benefits at the same time.

Maybe when you were young, you witnessed the way your father abused your mother and you were so hurt and swore never to get married. Many years have come and gone, and now, you are of age and wonder why no one is interested in marrying you. Negative words spoken especially in times of anger are very powerful and destructive. Your thoughts and words are very important. Do not allow negative thoughts to find a resting place in your mind. You need to steer clear from this harmful lifestyle.

Fear is another source of self-inflicted curse. To allow fear of the negative to have dominion and control over your life is to place your destiny under the curse. Let us look at the case of Job, who was well protected but did not know it.

> You have always put a wall of protection around him and his home and his property. You have made him prosper in everything he does. Look how rich he is! (Job 1:10 NLT)

You can see from the scripture that Job and all he had were well secured by God. Even the devil knew that quite well. Unfortunately, Job allowed fear to dictate the outcome of his future because he was not aware of the hedge God had built around about him and everything belonging to him. When you allow fear to nest upon your life, you have opened a way for the enemy to cause havoc. After the disaster that happened to Job, he confessed, "What I always feared has happened to me. What I dreaded has come true" (Job 3:25 NLT). Do not allow fear to take residence in your mind. Attack it like you would a rattlesnake! To be afraid is not a sin, but to live in fear is a sin.

—THE CURSE OF THE DEVIL

The devil is against everything that is good. One of his ways of bringing a curse upon humanity is to instigate or lure a person to do things contrary to the will of God. The children of Israel were a blessed nation. As they journeyed from Egypt to the Promised Land, no nation was strong enough to stop them. As they approached the land of Moab, the king heard of what Israel had done to other nations and was so scared, so he employed the services of Balaam, a mighty prophet, to curse the people of Israel. Unfortunately, he could not curse them even though he tried several times. The power of the blessing resisted him because the people of Israel were a nation blessed by God.

However, Balaam was able to counsel Balak to have his people mingle with the Israelites and influence them with their heathen lifestyle. This "caused the children of Israel, through the counsel of Balaam, to commit trespass against the Lord" (Numbers 31:16). The counsel was to lure them to do things contrary to God's instruction. The strategy was to cause the people to sin against God (that way, they would lose the force of the blessing and their protection) and thereby incur the wrath of God.

> While the Israelites were camped at Acacia Grove, some of the men defiled themselves by having sexual relations with local Moabite women. These women invited them to attend sacrifices to their gods, so the Israelites feasted with them and worshiped the gods of Moab. In this way, Israel joined in the worship of Baal of Peor, causing the LORD's anger to blaze against his people. (Numbers 25:1–3 NLT)

Behind every curse is the devil. You do not have to be evil to come under his curse. From the moment he made Adam to commit high treason, he took over the authority of the human race and became the god of this world. So as long as one is of this world and not in Christ Jesus, the devil can place a curse on such a person. Only the blessing of God can erase this form of curse.

> Christ hath redeemed us from the curse of the law, being made a curse for us: for it is written, Cursed is every one that hangeth on a tree: That the blessing of

Abraham might come on the Gentiles through Jesus Christ; that we might receive the promise of the Spirit through faith. (Galatians 3:13–14)

– THE CURSE OF GOD

This form of curse is the strongest of all curses. This is due to the fact that there is none stronger than God. When God places a curse upon a person, no one but God can undo the curse. Once again, the devil is the one that instigates or lures people to do things contrary to the will of God, thereby incurring the curse of God. "The curse of the Lord is in and on the house of the wicked" (Proverbs 3:33 AMPC). The way out of all kinds of curses is in Christ Jesus. Our redemption in Christ Jesus answers to all forms of curses. Have a change of mind and turn over your life to God. Once this is done, you are discharged from all your offences. The Lord personally takes over your case.

> Shall the prey be taken from the mighty, or the lawful captive delivered? But thus saith the Lord, Even the captives of the mighty shall be taken away, and the prey of the terrible shall be delivered: for I will contend with him that contendeth with thee, and I will save thy children. And I will feed them that oppress thee with their own flesh; and they shall be drunken with their own blood, as with sweet wine: and all flesh shall know that I the Lord am thy Savior and thy Redeemer, the mighty One of Jacob. (Isaiah 49:24–26)

Even if you are lawfully captured by the enemy, the mercy of God has been extended to everyone in Christ Jesus. The moment you take a stand and surrender to Jesus, God takes over your battles and contends with the enemy for your freedom.

As children of God in Christ Jesus, we have been set free from all these curses listed above. But out of ignorance, negligence, or willful disobedience to the word of God, one may automatically open the door to any of these curses, and the force of evil begins to dominate such a life. Some have been under the influence of a curse for so long that they have ignorantly concluded that the curse is stronger than the blessing. No! The blessing is your way out of every form of curse. No matter what the curse you have allowed upon your life, the blessing of Abraham will swallow it up. All you need to do is turn to God in genuine repentance. That's all the Lord requires from you—a change of mind and to stop thinking that the curse is stronger than the word of the all-powerful Lord.

Among the four curses listed above, the curse of God is the most powerful. Yet God in His love and mercy has absorbed all forms of curses in Jesus Christ.

> Who shall bring any charge against God's elect when it is God Who justifies that is, Who puts us in right relation to Himself? Who shall come forward and accuse or impeach those whom God has chosen? Will God, Who acquits us? Who is there to condemn us? Will Christ Jesus (the Messiah), Who died, or rather Who was raised from the dead, Who is at the right hand of God actually pleading as He intercedes for us? (Romans 8:33–34 AMPC)

Jesus is the one who died for you; no one has the authority to place a curse on you. The one who has the final say is God, and Jesus is right now at His right hand interceding for you!

— A BLESSED PERSON CANNOT BE CURSED

> How shall I curse, whom God hath not cursed? or how shall I defy, whom the Lord hath not defied? (Numbers 23:8)

The blessing upon your life cannot be overturned by any curse. To put it mildly, a blessed person *cannot* be cursed.

> God is not a man, that he should lie; neither the son of man, that he should repent: hath he said, and shall he not do it? or hath he spoken, and shall he not make it good? Behold, I have received commandment to bless: and he hath blessed; and I cannot reverse it. (Numbers 23:19–20)

To curse a man whom God has blessed is a waste of time. In fact, the person trying to curse him will end up being accursed. Why? The scripture records that God will "Curse him that curseth thee." When God created Adam and Eve, He blessed them as recorded in Genesis 1:27–28:

> So God created man in his own image, in the image of God created he him; male and female created he them. And God blessed them, and God said unto them, Be fruitful, and multiply, and replenish the earth, and subdue it: and have dominion over the fish of the sea, and over the fowl of the air, and over every living thing that moveth upon the earth.

Here we see that God blessed Adam and Eve, as He pronounced the blessing upon them. In chapter 3 of the book of Genesis, the unimaginable happened. Adam knowingly disobeyed God and thus committed high treason, and God pronounced a curse.

> Unto Adam he said, because thou hast hearkened unto the voice of thy wife, and hast eaten of the tree, of which I commanded thee, saying, Thou shalt not eat of it: cursed is the ground for thy sake; in sorrow shalt thou eat of it all the days of thy life. (Genesis 3:17)

Notice that God did not curse the man, whom He had declared blessed previously. Rather, He cursed the ground; here we see the mercy of God in operation. He didn't put a curse on him. You know why? We are made in His image and likeness, and God cannot curse Himself. The curse was on the ground, not on the man. There is a big difference between the man and the ground. If God will not curse the man He had blessed, who then can place a curse on you? Every curse is terminated and removed when the blessing comes upon you.

> Christ hath redeemed us from the curse of the law, being made a curse for us: for it is written, Cursed is every one that hangeth on a tree: That the blessing of Abraham might come on the Gentiles through Jesus Christ; that we might receive the promise of the Spirit through faith. (Galatians 3:13–14)

Your freedom has been paid for, and in the realm of the supernatural, you are free. It is time to enforce your freedom, for Christ took your place. You have been redeemed from every form of curse by the death of Jesus Christ. He paid for your liberty, and as He took our curse, He opened the gate of life that the blessing of Abraham might come on you and me.

– GOD IS NOW YOUR FATHER

These days a lot of believers are more conscious of the curse than the blessing. Unfortunately, some pulpit ministers have placed undue emphasis on the curse. Once a believer has a problem, these ministers will always link the issue to a curse. If that is the case with you, expect your freedom!

Jesus Christ took your place and carried your every curse on Him as He hung on the tree. He paid for your curse and in exchange credited your account with the blessing of Abraham (Galatians 3:13–14). The enemy can use your past and ignorance to torment your destiny and eventually destroy your life. But for the Christian, it ought not to be so. The very moment you gave your life to Jesus Christ, there was a switch in the realm of the spirit. There was a changeover, a total turnaround in terms of to whom you are now subject. You are now under a new authority and have been grafted into a new lineage. There is a new order. Before you gave your life to Christ, you were subject to the devil and were under his authority and domain. God was not your Father. Yes, He was not your Father. God created everyone, but He is not the Father of everyone. Jesus said so.

> For you are the children of your father the devil …
> (John 8:44 NLT)

You cannot be a child of the devil and at the same time a child of the heavenly Father. The moment you gave your life to Christ Jesus, God brought you into a new order or relationship with the Almighty, now as your Father! God is now with you and in you (John 14:17 NCV). You are now in the kingdom of light, having been delivered from the power of darkness, because all forms of curses are under the power of darkness.

> Giving thanks to the Father who has qualified us to be partakers of the inheritance of the saints in the light. He has delivered us from the power of darkness and conveyed us into the kingdom of the Son of His love, in whom we have redemption through His blood, the forgiveness of sins. (Colossians 1:12–14 NKJV)

You have been taken out of the kingdom of darkness. You are now in the kingdom of the Son of His love, and your sins are no more. You are now free from all your past sins. Satan is no more in charge; he has been dethroned. Legally speaking, God is now your Father! The word says, "As many as received him, to them gave he power to become the sons of God, even to them that believe on his name" (John 1:12). You have been born again into the greatest and most prestigious royal family in the universe!

The Spirit you received does not make you a slave, so that you live in fear again; "rather, the Spirit you received brought about your adoption to sonship. And by him we cry, 'Abba, Father'" (Romans 8:15 NIV).

— THE CHOICE IS YOURS

> My people are destroyed for lack of knowledge. Because you have rejected knowledge, I also will reject you. (Hosea 4:6 NKJV)

Know that the enemy can take advantage of your ignorance. Yes, you have been set free, but unless you know and embrace the truth, you may suffer the same fate as the person in the "world of darkness." Locate the truth, and allow the gospel to affect your entire life. One of the greatest men who walked the face of this earth, Archbishop Benson Idahosa, once said, "If you are affected by Christ, you cannot be afflicted by your past." This is the whole truth. To enable the blessing of Abraham to penetrate all aspects of your life, take the blessing and begin an active meditation on it. Expose your soul to the truth of the blessing of Abraham. When the truth is revealed to you, it should be practiced until it resonates from deep within you. Allow the Holy Spirit the opportunity to take you on a journey of a lifetime.

No matter how long a curse has been upon one's life, an encounter with Christ automatically extinguishes all forms of curses.

The self-inflicted curse, the curse of a man, the curse of the devil, and the curse of God are all swallowed by the death and resurrection of Jesus Christ. So you see that the blessing is stronger than the curse. Make your choice; no curse has the right to remain upon your life. Ignorantly you may have allowed the enemy to oppress you, but now you know the truth: Christ Jesus became a curse for you, that you might receive the blessing of Abraham. What is inside of you is a million times bigger than whatever curse the enemy can put on you.

Imagine trying to drain out the water from the Atlantic Ocean! Do you think the devil can do that? No, he can't do it. In the same way, the devil cannot put a curse on you. You are the blessed child of the most high God. You are loved and forgiven. The sacrificial blood of the Lamb has bestowed upon you the weight of God's glory. The glory of God upon you refers to God's favor upon you. It is not just favor but heavy favor, heavy enough to terminate every form of curse. Every force of evil comes to an end when the blessing comes upon your life. Every generational curse comes to an end, when the blessing is active and working in you.

The blessing is bigger than Father Abraham; in fact, the blessing is bigger than life. Jesus Christ is the blessing of Abraham!

In conclusion, remember that what controls or influences your spirit controls your present and future outcome in life. To control your spirit, you must ensure the content of your spirit. Your physical body is sustained by the food you eat, and in the same way, your spirit is kept and controlled by what you are feeding it with. The Bible is the primary source of right food for your spirit. Jeremiah the prophet penned these beautiful words: "Thy words were found, and I did eat them; and thy word was unto me the joy and rejoicing of mine heart: for I am called by thy name, O Lord God of hosts" (Jeremiah 15:16). After finding the word, he ate it, and it became the joy and strength of his spirit (heart). Again, in the book of Ezekiel 2:8–9, the Lord gave the same instruction: "But thou, son of man, hear what I say unto thee; Be not thou rebellious like that rebellious house: open thy mouth, and eat that I give thee. And when I looked, behold, an hand was sent unto me; and, lo, a roll of a book was therein." Paul the apostle instructs us to "Let the word spoken by Christ the Messiah have its home in your hearts and minds and dwell in you in all its richness…" (Colossians3:16 AMPC)

The truth in the Bible is to be eaten. That is, spend time to speak the word and pray the word as you meditate on it. This is the process by which Joshua was affected and influenced by the word and became a great leader (Joshua 1:8).

CHAPTER 4

SEARCHING FOR THE BLESSING

The Lord God planted a garden eastward in Eden; and there he put the man whom he had formed. (Genesis 2:8)

The garden of Eden is still as real today as it was back then in the book of Genesis, when God spoke to Adam and Eve. The garden of Eden is a perfect manifestation of the love and goodness of God. Eden was a place where there was no sickness, no disease, no lack or poverty. Everything they needed was thoroughly provided for. Adam and Eve had a desire for nothing else but God. Adam was king and master over everything created. This is what the blessing is capable of doing. Remember, when God created Adam and Eve, He pronounced the blessing on them. The blessing of Eden is still available today. It is called the blessing of Abraham or better still *the good news*! (We will talk about that later.)

Unfortunately, so many are searching for the blessing in the wrong places. I love telling this story of Ali Hafed from the book titled *Acres of Diamonds* by Russell H. Conwell.

— THE STORY OF ALI HAFED

The old guide told me that there once lived not far from the River Indus an ancient Persian by the name of Ali Hafed. He said that Ali

Hafed owned a very large farm, that he had orchards, grain-fields, and gardens, and that he loaned money at an interest and was a wealthy and contented man. He was contented because he was wealthy and wealthy because he was contented. One day, one of these ancient Buddhist priests and one of the wise men of the East visited that old Persian farmer. He sat down by the fire and told the old farmer how this world of ours was made, and then told him how diamond was made. ... Said the old priest, "A diamond is a congealed drop of sunlight." Now that is literally scientifically true, that a diamond is an actual deposit of carbon from the sun. The old priest told Ali Hafed that if he had one diamond the size of his thumb he could purchase the county, and if he had a mine of diamonds, he could place his children upon thrones through the influence of their great wealth.

Ali Hafed heard all about diamonds and how much they were worth, and he went to his bed that night a poor man. He had not lost anything, but he was poor because he was discontented and discontented because he feared he was poor. He said, "I want a mine of diamonds," and he lay awake all night.

Early in the morning, he sought out the priest. I know by experience that a priest is very cross when awakened early in the morning, and when he shook that old priest out of his dreams, Ali Hafed said to him: "Will you tell me where I can find diamonds?"

"Diamonds! What do you want with diamonds?"

"Why, I wish to be immensely rich."

"Well, then, go along and find them. That is all you have to do; go and find them, and then you have them."

"But I don't know where to go."

"Well, if you will find a river that runs through white sands, between high mountains, in those white sands you will always find diamonds."

"I don't believe there is any such river."

"Oh yes, there are plenty of them. All you have to do is to go and find them, and then you have them."

Said Ali Hafed, "I will go."

So he sold his farm, collected his money, left his family in charge of a neighbor, and went away in search of diamonds. He began his search, very clearly to my mind, at the Mountains of the Moon. Afterward he came around into Palestine, then wandered on into Europe, and at last when his money was all spent and he was in rags, wretchedness, and poverty, he stood on the shore of that bay at Barcelona, in Spain, when a great tidal wave came rolling in between the pillars of Hercules, and the poor, afflicted, suffering, dying man could not resist the awful temptation to cast himself into that incoming tide, and he sank beneath its foaming crest, never to rise in this life again …

The man who purchased Ali Hafed's farm one day led his camel into the garden to drink, and as that camel put its nose into the shallow water of that garden brook, Ali Hafed's successor noticed a curious flash of light from the white sands of the stream. He pulled out a black stone having an eye of light reflecting all the hues of the rainbow. He took the pebble into the house and put it on the mantel that covers the central fires and forgot all about it.

A few days later this same old priest came in to visit Ali Hafed's successor, and the moment he opened that drawing room door, he saw that flash of light on the mantel, and he rushed up to it, and shouted: "Here is a diamond! Has Ali Hafed returned?"

"Oh no, Ali Hafed has not returned, and that is not a diamond. That is nothing but a stone we found right out here in our own garden."

"But," said the priest, "I tell you I know a diamond when I see it. I know without a doubt that it is a diamond."

Then together they rushed out into that old garden and stirred up the white sands with their fingers, and lo! There came up other more beautiful and valuable gems than the first. "Thus," said the guide to me and friends, it is historically true, "was discovered the diamond-mine of Golconda, the most magnificent diamondmine in all the history of humankind, excelling the Kimberly itself. The Kohinoor and the Orlo of the crown jewels of England and Russia, the largest on earth, came from that mine."

— YOU HAVE EVERYTHING INSIDE YOU ————————

This story always reminds me that whatever we are looking for out there is inside of us. Some have left behind a great mine of "diamonds" in their home country and gone abroad looking for greener pasture, only to be roaming around, doing nothing tangible. If God has not given you a go-ahead, stay put in your country. Remember Isaac? He was about to check out of the land to Egypt, the America of their time, due to the famine. However, God told him to stay in the land and he obeyed, and God blessed him really good. Find out the mind of God before you take off. Ali Hafed went away looking for diamonds and eventually died without finding diamonds. Meanwhile, diamonds were in the stream that passed through his property. Inside his farmland were mines of diamonds. Do not undermine the talent you have. Everything that will make you great has been deposited in you.

Today God is still planting the garden of the blessing in the hearts of Christians, so we need to redirect our search. Inside every Christian is embedded the source of the blessing of Abraham. According to the word of God, "His divine power hath given unto us all things that pertain unto life and godliness, through the knowledge of him that hath called us to glory and virtue" (2 Peter 1:3). Everything that makes for life and godly living has been given to you and me. "Blessed be the God and Father of our Lord Jesus Christ, who has blessed us with every spiritual blessing in the heavenly places in Christ" (Ephesians 1:3 NKJV). Every spiritual blessing that has been deposited in you is designed to be tapped via the word.

> Who being the brightness of his glory, and the express image of his person, and upholding all things by the word of his power, when he had by himself purged our sins, sat down on the right hand of the Majesty on high. (Hebrews 1:3)

God upholds all things by the word of His power. God works with His word. Get into the word and find out what He will have you do.

Your destiny depends on what you find in the pages of the Bible, and the wonderful part of it is that the Holy Spirit is there to lead and guide you into the truth. God knows where the blessing is and will not lead you in a wrong way. Every instruction from the Lord carries a blessing. He leads us in the right path. God told Isaac what to do and he obeyed the God of his father, and the blessing made him the envy of the whole nation. Get into the word; it is the right place to start your search. Read and study with a heart ready to receive instructions from the Lord. All you need is a divine instruction.

> And the Lord appeared unto him, and said, Go not down into Egypt; dwell in the land which I shall tell thee of: Sojourn in this land, and I will be with thee, and will bless thee; for unto thee, and unto thy seed, I will give all these countries, and I will perform the oath which I sware unto Abraham thy father. (Genesis 26:2–3)

God promised: "I will perform the oath (word)." God performs His word and His promises. Jeremiah 1:12 confirms that He will perform His word "for I will hasten my word to perform it." The Lord always works with His word. Remember, creating the blessing lies deep within the content of the gospel deposited in your spirit, which you draw out via the words you speak.

—WHAT IS THE GOSPEL?

The gospel of the kingdom that Jesus Christ came to introduce was first preached to Abraham. Galatians 3:8 says, "And the scripture, foreseeing that God would justify the heathen through faith, preached before the gospel unto Abraham, saying, In thee shall all nations be blessed." The gospel is the good news: that the blessing of Abraham that is the same blessing pronounced on Adam and Eve at the beginning is available to every Christian in Christ Jesus. This is the good news! The blessing of Abraham is the gospel of Jesus Christ.

— YOU HAVE BEEN ENTRUSTED WITH THE BLESSING —

> But just as we have been approved by God to be entrusted with the glad tidings (the Gospel), so we speak not to please men but to please God, Who tests our hearts expecting them to be approved. (1 Thessalonians 2:4 AMPC)

Christians have been entrusted with the glad tidings, which is the gospel. The gospel is so glorious and important to God that He personally came down and preached it to His friend Abraham. We are called to embrace the gospel with joy and run with it.

Winning souls to God is a matter of sharing the glad tidings; we must let people know that the same blessing conferred upon Abraham can be theirs, as they trust in the finished work of Jesus Christ. They need not live in darkness anymore, for the curse, and sins and works of darkness, have been dealt with. Indeed, the gospel is good news. No wonder Paul the apostle could boast, "I am not ashamed of the gospel of Christ: for it is the power of God unto salvation to everyone that believeth" (Romans 1:16). The reason some Christians are ashamed of the gospel is because they are ignorant of its power to save souls from sin, Satan, sickness, and spiritual dearth. The blessing of Abraham that God has packaged for us has the elastic capacity to enrich your family from generation to generation until the return of Jesus Christ. The gospel is the blessing of the Lord and has the capacity to transform lives. You were created to rule your circumstances no matter how dark your situation may be. God has placed within you the ability to dominate your situation and come out on top.

─ BEGIN YOUR SEARCH IN THE SPIRIT REALM ─────

Out of the spiritual realm comes forth the physical. It was so in the beginning, and God has not changed the order. First of all, there was a spirit world before the physical world that can be seen and touched. The word is the gateway to the spirit realm, and this means that every search for the blessing of Abraham should begin from the word of His grace. Everything you can think of is in the realm of the spirit. Success, failure, and all the other things are there in the realm of the spirit. God began the creation of the world from the Spirit realm; He spoke the word. According to Hebrews 11:3 (AMPC), the world was called into existence by the word: "By faith we understand that the worlds during the successive ages were framed (fashioned, put in order, and equipped for their intended purpose) by the word of God, so that what we see was not made out of things which are visible." The world we live in today was created by the word of God. He created things out of the unseen realm. The word of God holds and controls the unseen realm of the spirit. Speaking to the believers in Ephesus, Paul commended us to God and to the word of His grace, which has the capacity to make us grow and deliver to us the blessings of Abraham.

> And now, brethren, I commend you to God, and to
> the word of his grace, which is able to build you up,
> and to give you an inheritance among all them which
> are sanctified. (Acts 20:32)

Every search in matters of life should begin with the word, and as you locate it, lay hold of it. Then step out into the physical world. You will discover that God has made arrangements in conformity with your discovery far beyond "all that we ask or think, according to the power that worketh in us." You must permit the word to generate power in you. Therefore, your search for the blessing of the Lord must begin with the word. Remember, it is written, "God upholds all things by the word of His power!" (Hebrews 1:3).

CHAPTER 5

ENJOYING THE BLESSING

God, who giveth us richly all things to enjoy. (1 Timothy 6:17)

THE SIMPLICITY OF FAITH

Faith in God is vital and necessary for you and me to enjoy the blessing of Abraham. Faith in the word of God is not as difficult as many claim. Faith in the word of God is simple and easy, but as simple as faith is, the power is tremendous. The power of faith will put you right into the blessing of the Lord. Your faith, when put to work, can remove mountains that stand on your way. It will enrich your life and enrich your bank account. Everything about God is simple and straightforward. Human beings have introduced all manner of complications into the gospel.

> But I fear, lest by any means, as the serpent beguiled Eve through his subtilty, so your minds should be corrupted from the simplicity that is in Christ. (2 Corinthians 11:3)

Paul the apostle warns that we should not allow our minds to be corrupted from the simplicity that is in the gospel, comparing it with how the serpent deceived Eve. The serpent took advantage of the simple instruction given to Adam and Eve and twisted Eve's mind.

Questions such as, "Does God mean exactly what the word says? Is that all you have to do?" If you are not careful, such statements are meant to derail your faith. The answer to both questions should be yes. God means exactly what He says, and what He has asked you to do is all you need to do. The Lord will not ask you to do something you do not have the capacity or ability to do. It would be unrighteous for the holy God to ask you to do something for which you do not have the capacity or ability. Taking God at His word is what faith is all about. Obeying God's word will fix any problems or challenges facing you right now. Learn to take God by His word. It's that simple. Maybe in your life, you have many questions but few answers or no answer at all. Living by faith in God's word will give answers to life's most challenging issues.

Your faith in the blessing will fix you as a person. You may feel inadequate at first, and that is permissible. Do not give up; just trust in God and in His word. Keep holding on to His word, and live a joyful life. God makes a way where there seems to be no way. Faith in God was what settled Abraham and Sarah. They were old and had passed the age of childbearing and therefore felt inadequate at first due to their circumstances. Most people become like that when they rule themselves out of God's blessing due to one limitation or another.

> Then Abraham fell upon his face, and laughed, and said in his heart, Shall a child be born unto him that is an hundred years old? and shall Sarah, that is ninety years old, bear? Now Abraham and Sarah were old and well stricken in age; and it ceased to be with Sarah after the manner of women. Therefore Sarah laughed within herself, saying, after I am waxed old shall I have pleasure, my lord being old also? (Genesis 17:17, 18:11–12)

From the above scriptures, it is obvious that they both felt it was impossible for the promised child to come forth. Abraham must have thought God was joking. Why? They were busy looking at themselves;

their focus was not on God. Physically speaking, they were too old to have a baby, and they had concluded that. Actually, they had a good laugh at God because God's word to them was ridiculous. Did you notice that Abraham tried to talk God out of the promised child Isaac, as God unveiled the plan? God said,

> "I will change the name of Sarai, your wife, to Sarah. I will bless her and give her a son, and you will be the father. She will be the mother of many nations. Kings of nations will come from her." Abraham bowed face down on the ground and laughed. He said to himself, "Can a man have a child when he is a hundred years old? Can Sarah give birth to a child when she is ninety?" Then Abraham said to God, "**Please let Ishmael be the son you promised.**" (Genesis 17:15–18 NCV, emphasis mine)

Unbelief is a very dangerous thing. All the while, one would have thought Abraham was waiting on God. But the truth is, God was working on His friend to change his thinking and put his faith in Him. God was talking of Isaac to Abraham, and meanwhile Abraham was thinking of Ishmael. In fact, he suggested to God to forget Isaac and that Ishmael should be the promised son. Can you imagine that? We have to come to the same level with the word of God. Take God at His word. Do not allow your situation to take your focus away from God's word. To have faith in God means to take God at His word.

When Abraham and Sarah realized that God was serious about His promise, they stopped laughing and got focused on the word, and you know what? They did exactly what Jesus said we should do—*have faith in God*!

> And Jesus answering saith unto them, Have faith in God. For verily I say unto you, That whosoever shall say unto this mountain, Be thou removed, and be thou cast into the sea; and shall not doubt in his

heart, but shall believe that those things which he saith shall come to pass; he shall have whatsoever he saith. Therefore I say unto you, What things soever ye desire, when ye pray, believe that ye receive them, and ye shall have them. (Mark 11:22–24)

To have faith in God is to take Him at His word. When they saw that God was not wavering, Sarah and her husband adjusted their faith, and I think we all need to adjust our faith. Like Dr. Sam Amaga will say, "Go and dust your faith." We all need to dust our faith. Faith requires focus in order to produce the result viz:

- The word or the promise
- Believe the word
- Speak the word
- Act the word

— THE WORD OR THE PROMISE

To know or have the word or the promise of the Lord is important. Abraham laid hold of the word that was spoken to him, and his faith came alive "according to that which was spoken, so shall thy seed be." Faith is elusive where the will of the Father is not known. Once you know the will of the Father, faith comes alive with passion. Your faith is only strengthened where the will of God is known and embraced. It is not enough to know the word of the Lord; you have to embrace it. In Deuteronomy 29:9, Moses instructed the nation of Israel, "Keep therefore the words of this covenant, and do them, that ye may prosper in all that ye do." God wants you to excel in all you do, and He tells us how: keep therefore the words of this covenant, and do them. The word has to become your constant companion in life. Know it, keep it, and do it. Make it your own, as if God spoke it to you directly, with your name tag on it.

On a daily basis, discipline yourself to live in the word and the word in you (John 15:4–7). By so doing, you have wrapped yourself completely with His light.

> My son, keep your father's commands, and don't forget your mother's teaching. Keep their words in mind forever as though you had them tied around your neck. They will guide you when you walk. They will guard you when you sleep. They will speak to you when you are awake. These commands are like a lamp; this teaching is like a light. And the correction that comes from them will help you have life. (Proverbs 6:20–23 NCV)

This is the best way to enjoy the blessing of Abraham. The word becomes your Shepherd as He leads, guides, and speaks to you. The word of God is the way out of every crisis.

Jeremiah was down and frustrated, but when he found the appropriate word, his joy came alive. He said it this way: "Thy words were found, and I did eat them; and thy word was unto me the joy and rejoicing of mine heart: for I am called by thy name, O Lord God of hosts" (Jeremiah 15:16). The good Lord has made several avenues for us to find the word. Sometimes when you are reading the Bible or a book, listening to a pastor or preacher, or just talking with someone, you can always find the word. For now, there is no scarcity of the word. The most important thing is to locate the word that promises to meet your particular desire, and then feast on it.

Joy is a prerequisite for your victory. Feasting on the promises of God generates joy in you, and when joy has found a home in your heart, you will begin to draw blessings from the storehouse of the Lord.

> Therefore with joy shall ye draw water out of the wells of salvation. (Isaiah 12:3)

The blessing will only respond to you if there is joy in your heart.

The promise of God will begin to benefit you as you allow the force of joy to flow out from your inside. God will answer you in the joy of your heart. The word is the solution to all the problems of humanity. The solution is in the word. Locate the word, and start eating it.

BELIEVE THE WORD

We have established the truth that God blessed Abraham and his descendants throughout all generations, and the blessing was passed from Abraham to Isaac, to Jacob, and then to us.

You *must* know and embrace the truth, that it is God's good pleasure to establish the blessing of Abraham in your life. The wisdom of achieving this is simply to believe, because believing is the access to everything in the kingdom of God. Without believing, nothing works in the kingdom of God. From Abraham, Isaac, and Jacob, down to everyone who made an impact with the Lord, they all believed. No matter how big the dream is, you have to believe it is possible, just like Mary did. "And blessed is she that believed: for there shall be a performance of those things which were told her from the Lord" (Luke 1:45). Believing leads to having. When we release belief, we receive that for which we believe. There will always be a performance of the blessings to those who believe.

In his daily devotional, Kenneth Copeland wrote about the power of believing. "It's the way we tap into the very power of Almighty God." Most of us know that, but few do exactly that kind of believing. We don't know how to put it into action. Actually, it's so simple that it's startling. It's as simple as saying, "I believe I receive." Something happens in your spirit when you say those words. I don't understand how, but it does. I don't understand how my digestive system knows what to do when I swallow something, but it does. All I have to do is take a bite of food and it goes to work. I don't have to make it happen. I don't have to feel it happen. It just happens. That's the way the body is made. In much the same way, when you feed on God's precious promises and "swallow" them into your spirit by saying, "I believe I receive," faith is released. You don't have to make it happen. You don't have to feel it happen. It just happens. The reborn spirit is made that way. When you constantly say with your mouth, "I believe I receive my healing" or "I believe I receive my financial needs met," and then quote the scriptures that back those things, faith is released to bring power to bear on those needs. As Dr. Kenneth Hagin says, you need to keep the switch of faith turned on. And Gloria and I have discovered that speaking out that phrase, "I believe I receive," is one way to do it. We say it when we pray. We say it when we praise God. We say it when we read the word. We say it especially in the face of darkness when it looks like we're not receiving. When everything looks the worst, we say it the loudest. I believe I receive! Do you want to activate your faith today? Then make these four key words the most important words in your vocabulary. Use them every day. You'll soon discover, just as we did … they work."

When you have found the word of His grace, practice the power of belief. Do not toss it aside, saying, "This can happen for Mr. So and Mrs. So, but not for me." No. The promise is for everyone who will believe. Until Abraham changed his perspective and believed, the word could not profit him. It won't cost you anything to believe. You have nothing to lose but everything to gain. When you believe, the blessing is activated. On the other hand, unbelief will deactivate the blessing. Jesus went about doing good and healing all who were oppressed of the devil. But when he came to Nazareth, where He grew up, they did not believe in Him.

> And he did not many mighty works there because of
> their unbelief. (Matthew 13:58)

This is Jesus; He could not do many mighty works because of their unbelief. When we believe, we enter into the plan and blessing of the Lord for us. No matter how big your dreams, just believe God is much more than able. The scripture says:

That famous promise God gave Abraham—that he and his children would possess the earth—was not given because of something Abraham did or would do. It was based on God's decision to put everything together for him, whom Abraham then entered when he believed. (Romans 4:13 MSG)

To believe is a miracle. It was Abraham's belief that thrust him right into God's plan for his life. Suddenly, he realized it was not by power or intellect, but by the Spirit of the Lord.

And blessed is she that believed: for there shall be a performance of those things which were told her from the Lord. (Luke 1:45)

There is a demonstration of power when you believe. Mary believed the unimaginable and unthinkable. You too can believe, and as you do, there shall be a performance of the word you believe. Abraham believed and saw, and so you will also! In the world it is commonly said "seeing is believing" but in the word or the kingdom of God, *believing is seeing*! When you believe, you will see what you believe. Again and again, Jesus placed emphasis on our believing in God. He said it this way: "all things are possible to him who believes" (Mark 9:23). You have what it takes to believe. The enemy will contest your right; he will challenge your belief, and that is where prayer comes in. You must stand with the word to confront the enemy and resist all doubts and fears that the enemy is using to attack your mind. Our great aim in life is to believe Jesus Christ and His words. Laboring also in the word will produce a supernatural harvest of the evidence of what we have believed. Therefore, your greatest work as a believer is to labor or work at your heart to believe the word of God.

When you believe the promise of God with a high expectancy, the Almighty goes into operation, working behind the scenes to bring to pass your desired expectation.

— SPEAK THE WORD ————————————————

Once Abraham and Sarah believed the word, they began speaking it. They believed that the Lord's promise would come to pass in their lives. What you say with your mouth is as important as what you believe.

> For verily I say unto you, That whosoever shall say unto this mountain, Be thou removed, and be thou cast into the sea; and shall not doubt in his heart, but shall believe that those things which he saith shall come to pass; he shall have whatsoever he saith. (Mark 11:23)

Your blessing is tied to what you believe, and much more what you say. Look at the scripture above; four times the word *say* is used in connection with bringing to pass the desires of your heart. Learn to speak only what you want. Monitor the words that you speak. If you don't like the words coming out of your mouth, or you do not like the harvest from your life, then change the source of your information. To speak right words, start reading the Bible and good books. It won't be long before you start speaking like your heavenly Father, who gives life to the dead and calls into being things that were not (Romans 4:17). To enjoy the blessing of Abraham, you have to keep speaking the blessing. Your result in life is directly equal to the words you believe and speak through your mouth. So do not keep quiet; open your mouth and say what you want to see, not your experience, but what you desire.

> And since we have the same spirit of faith, according to what is written, "I believed and therefore I spoke," we also believe and therefore speak. (2 Corinthians 4:13 NKJV)

We have the same spirit with Abraham, David, and Paul. These men believed and spoke what they believed. By faith begin to speak what you want to see. You will be rewarded by what you say, whether good or bad. "People will be rewarded for what they say; they will be rewarded by how they speak" (Proverbs 18:20 NCV). Choose to speak good about your destiny and you will reap the harvest. "Words kill, words give life; they're either poison or fruit— you choose" (Proverbs 18:21 MSG). Choose life and you and your entire family will experience the blessing. You can never speak too much of the word. Yes. You can never speak too much of God's word. Indeed, you should use every opportunity to speak the word.

In the year 2006, one of the fathers in the gospel gave several thousand USdollars into the work of the gospel of Jesus Christ. I recently saw an article he delivered in the year 2007, where he spoke on the secret of his wealth and this is what he said, "if you have not said the word (referring to God's promise concerning your need) about 500 times a day, you have not started." Look at that! That sounds like someone who means business. How desperately do you want a manifestation of God's blessing upon your life? We ought to pay attention to this wisdom key from an exemplary father who has been a man of integrity over the years. Speaking God's word in secret and in public will embolden your faith.

The woman with the issue of blood for twelve years showed us how powerful and important the words you speak consistently work. We are told in Mark 5:27–28 (AMPC) when "she had heard the reports concerning Jesus, and she came up behind Him in the throng and touched His garment, For she kept saying, If I only touch His garments, I shall be restored to health." Did you take note that she kept saying, "If I only touch His garments, I shall be restored to health." For how long she kept saying it, I do not know. But it was very clear she did not say it once or occasionally. All through the day, it could be under your breath, so speak your expectation.

Start speaking the word. When your thoughts and words are dominated by God's word, no matter the situation or the opposition, the blessing is bound to flow. Negative words have no place in the kingdom of God. Your life today is the harvest of all the words you have spoken to date. Instead of speaking your experience, start speaking your expectation. Keep your faith and eyes steady on the word, and let it flow from your mouth. One touch of God's favor can turn things around, so don't give up or get discouraged because you do not see anything happening, God is working behind the scenes, making the necessary arrangements (1 Samuel 1:19 MSG). Please, do not interfere with what the Lord is doing by speaking wrong or negative words. Every difficulty is only temporal. Keep believing, keep doing what is right, and keep speaking right words. Live daily with expectancy. Breakthrough is coming your way.

— ACT THE WORD

First locate the word as it relates to your need, and then believe it in your heart and start speaking what you want to see. You will begin to see your desires.

> Therefore I say unto you, What things soever ye desire, when ye pray, believe that ye receive them, and ye shall have them. (Mark 11:24)

Lay hold on the promise and refuse to give up. Some gave up before they started. To claim you believe that God is almighty and can do all things, and therefore that you are leaving it all up to Him, is as good as giving up. You need to stand and fight the good fight of faith by believing and speaking. Faith is the act of God and human working together for the release of divine destinies. Therefore, you cannot leave it up to God. You need to play your part. "Therefore I say unto you What things soever ye desire, when ye pray, believe that ye receive them, and ye shall have them" (Mark 11:24). The Greek word translated "receive" in the scripture above means to take, to get hold of, to receive to oneself—to seize. Remember that when Abraham believed, nothing may have happened to him physically to suggest that there was a change. He was still old; Sarah was still the same person. Nothing had changed. But on the inside, something had happened because he had allowed his spirit and mind to seize the promise. It was not a physical thing. It was the blessing at work, which made both Abraham and Sarah begin to think, speak, and act as if that promise was already done and that is faith. To receive the blessing, faith is required, and by faith, it means that you refuse to put your attention on your inadequacies; rather you focus your attention on the promises of God. For Abraham, he refused to consider his body that was now old or the deadness of Sarah's womb. He chose to believe the words of the blessing.

We have already noted that a blessed person cannot be cursed. God cannot curse a person He has blessed. Since God will not and cannot curse His child in Christ Jesus, then there is no human being born of a woman or a devil anywhere who is strong enough to place a curse on you. A man who is operating under the blessing will prosper in every department of his life. All that God is asking of you is to obey what He asked you to do, "If you follow them exactly, you will be successful in everything you do" (Joshua 1:7 NCV). To act on the word is to accept as the final authority what the word says rather than what your situation or opinion says. As long as your eyes are focused on your situation, you will be mocked, ridiculed, and tormented. Hannah, who had been barren for so long, found herself in that kind of situation that brought bitterness into her life, but then she decided to do something about it by acting on the word of God.

> She continued in prayer before God, Eli was watching her closely. Hannah was praying in her heart, silently. Her lips moved, but no sound was heard. Eli jumped to the conclusion that she was drunk. He approached her and said, "You're drunk! How long do you plan to keep this up? Sober up, woman!" Hannah said, "Oh no, sir—please! I'm a woman hard used. I haven't been drinking. Not a drop of wine or beer. The only thing I've been pouring out is my heart, pouring it out to God. Don't for a minute think I'm a bad woman.

It's because I'm so desperately unhappy and in such pain that I've stayed here so long." Eli answered her, "Go in peace. And may the God of Israel give you what you have asked of him.""Think well of me— and pray for me!" she said, and went her way. Then she ate heartily, her face radiant. Up before dawn, they worshiped God and returned home to Ramah. Elkanah slept with Hannah his wife, and God began making the necessary arrangements in response to what she had asked. Before the year was out, Hannah had conceived and given birth to a son. She named him Samuel, explaining, "I asked God for him."(1 Samuel 1:12-20 MSG)

You need to do what Hannah did. After she prayed, there was a change of focus and attitude. This is what it means to act on the word of God. Scripture says she became full of joy, and it reflected on her face: she was radiant because she was confident in the power of God to answer her prayer. So she acted as if everything was all right, and indeed, everything was all right, as she conceived and gave birth to Samuel and five other children (1 Samuel 2:21).

CHAPTER 6

STAY CONNECTED TO THE BLESSING

The blessing of the LORD makes one rich, And He adds no sorrow with it. (Proverbs 10:22 NKJV)

There is no doubt that it is the blessing of the Lord that makes one rich. It is not your job or whatever you are doing that makes you rich. There are others doing the same thing, and they are not on the same level as you are. Let me say it again: your job is only a channel for God to bring the Lord's blessing into your life. For every child of God, there is a blessing upon your life the moment you embrace Jesus Christ as your Lord and Savior; in the realm of the spirit, there is a supernatural transformation that takes place in your favor. With your salvation comes the package of the blessing of Abraham.

In other for you to start enjoying the blessing of the Lord, you have to stay connected to God. Your connection to the blessing is achieved through your daily dependence on God and His word.

— OBEDIENCE TO GOD

If they obey and serve him, they shall spend their days in prosperity, and their years in pleasures. But if they obey not, they shall perish by the sword, and they shall die without knowledge. (Job 36:11–12)

God earnestly desires that you spend your days in prosperity, and your years in abundant pleasures. Your entire future (in the blessing of Abraham) depends on your present or next step of obedience with God. Some steps of obedience can be major while some are minor. With God, whether major or minor, both are important and necessary for your promotion. May you never miss that minor or major step of obedience! We have to fully trust Him and obey His instructions in small or big issues, even when we do not understand what He is doing. Every instruction the Lord gives will always be in agreement with His word. Always crosscheck if you are not sure.

– ABRAHAMS OBEDIENCE

Obedience is a powerful key to the blessing of Abraham. Do not give up, never give up, and keep on going. Keep doing what you know to be true according to God's word. Your blessing cannot be stopped. God spoke and gave Abraham instructions, and he obeyed. "So Abram departed, as the Lord had spoken unto him" (Genesis 12:4). Once again, God tested and proved Abraham's obedience. He was asked to take his only son Isaac to a particular mountain, which God would tell him.

> When they came to the place of which God had told him, Abraham built an altar there; then he laid the wood in order and bound Isaac his son and laid him on the altar on the wood. And Abraham stretched forth his hand and took hold of the knife to slay his son. But the Angel of the Lord called to him from heaven and said, Abraham, Abraham! He answered, here I am. And He said, do not lay your hand on the lad or do anything to him; for now I know that you fear and revere God, since you have not held back from Me or begrudged giving Me your son, your only son. (Genesis 22:9-12 AMPC)

You will agree with me that this is one of the toughest and most fearful tests a person will have to go through. Abraham wasted no time, and neither did he call a meeting to debate the issue. He set out immediately to obey one of the most terrifying instructions of his life: to slay Isaac, the only son whom he loved. Take note; this is his only son as far as heaven is concerned. It takes the love of God in your heart to be able to sacrifice the only and most precious thing you have for the kingdom of God. Every little or big step of obedience is important to the one who gave the instruction. Do yourself a huge favor; obey every instruction from the Lord. The Bible is the word of God, and it is full of instructions for daily, healthy, victorious, and prosperous living in every area of life.

— MAJOR OR MINOR DISOBEDIENCE —

Sometimes what seems to be a minor act of disobedience can result in long-term misery in one's life. You are to do everything within your power to obey God, but when you miss it, ask for forgiveness immediately. Settle every wrongdoing by asking God to wipe it away. Do not wait for tomorrow. Delayed repentance and confession may be too late. Remember, "if we confess our sins, he is faithful and just to forgive us our sins, and to cleanse us from all unrighteousness" (1 John 1:9). One act of disobedience can terminate your destiny. It happened to Moses. The greatest desire of Moses was to take the Israelites into the Promised Land. For forty years he had labored night and day, for the land God promised was flowing with milk and honey. Unfortunately, Moses did not make it. He missed part of the blessing of Abraham because, under tremendous pressure from the people he was leading, he lost his temper, got angry, and disobeyed the instruction of the Lord. The Israelites were a tough set of people as at that time. They practically blamed Moses for everything in their lives.

> Now there was no water for the congregation, and they assembled together against Moses and Aaron. And

the people contended with Moses, and said, Would that we had died when our brethren died in the plague before the Lord! And why have you brought up the congregation of the Lord into this wilderness, that we should die here, we and our livestock? And why have you made us come up out of Egypt to bring us into this evil place? It is no place of grain or of figs or of vines or of pomegranates. And there is no water to drink. (Numbers 20:2–5 AMPC)

Moses cried to God, and God told him what to do.

The Lord said to Moses; Take the rod, and assemble the congregation, you and Aaron your brother, and tell the rock before their eyes to give forth its water, and you shall bring forth to them water out of the rock; so you shall give the congregation and their livestock drink. (Numbers 20:7–8 AMPC)

Moses had a problem, which we must all guard against. He allowed anger to gain access into his life. Though his anger was not directed at God, but at the people he was leading, it eventually led him into disobeying God's instruction.

And Moses and Aaron assembled the congregation before the rock and Moses said to them, Hear now, you rebels; must we bring you water out of this rock? And Moses lifted up his hand and with his rod he smote the rock twice. And the water came out abundantly, and the congregation drank, and their livestock. (Numbers 20:10–11 AMPC)

The instruction was to tell the rock to provide water. Instead of speaking to the rock, Moses struck the rock. His anger started showing in his words: as he called God's people "you rebels" and then with anger, he struck the rock twice. Water came out of the rock for the people to drink and for their livestock also. They were satisfied and happy, but for Moses the case was different. He realized he had disobeyed God. The Lord spoke to him and said: "Because ye believed me not, to sanctify me in the eyes of the children of Israel, therefore ye shall not bring this congregation into the land which I have given them" (Numbers 20:12). It is important to note that God did not say anything to Moses about the consequence of disobeying that one simple instruction to speak and not to strike. One wished that *Moses knew his future rested on that one simple step of obedience.*

Some Christians have this attitude "I will just yield to my flesh and repent later" with the hope that 1 John 1:9 will avail for them. No matter how small any instruction seems to you, it is very important to the Lord. The consequences can be very hard to bear. For Moses it ended his destiny.

> The Lord spake unto Moses that selfsame day, saying, Get thee up into this mountain Abarim, unto mount Nebo, which is in the land of Moab, that is over against Jericho; and behold the land of Canaan, which I give unto the children of Israel for a possession: And die in the mount whither thou goest up, and be gathered unto thy people; as Aaron thy brother died in mount Hor, and was gathered unto his people: Because ye trespassed against me among the children of Israel at the waters of Meribah-Kadesh, in the wilderness of Zin; because ye sanctified me not in the midst of the children of Israel. Yet thou shalt see the land before thee; but thou shalt not go thither unto the land which I give the children of Israel. (Deuteronomy 32:48–52)

Moses pleaded with God to allow him to get to the land, but the Lord refused. All God granted him was to see the land, but not to enter. Moses's greatest desire was to lead God's people into the

Promised Land. This was all Moses wanted on this side of heaven: to step into the land flowing with milk and honey.

> The Lord said unto him, "This is the land which I sware unto Abraham, unto Isaac, and unto Jacob, saying, I will give it unto thy seed: I have caused thee to see it with thine eyes, but thou shalt not go over thither. So Moses the servant of the Lord died there in the land of Moab, according to the word of the Lord." (Deuteronomy 34:4–5)

That is a very sobering account. It demonstrated just how serious disobedience can be. Moses died! It was not old age or any form of sickness or disease that ended his life; rather it was disobedience that was provoked by anger. *If anger did this to one of God's choicest servant leader,* imagine what can happen to you and me. The devil cannot hurt you in the blessing, but you can hurt yourself if you follow the devil's suggestion.

— AVOID MURMURING AND COMPLAINING ————

Before you were created, God had determined to bless you abundantly. It is not because of what you have done or who you are. It is as a result of God's unconditional love that He blesses you extravagantly. The Lord has already set you up to be blessed. All you have to do is believe. Instead of believing the promise of God, a lot of believers doubt their own ability to enter into the blessing of Abraham. Due to doubt, fear, and unbelief, they are frustrated, and the next thing is that murmuring and complaining become their companions.

— THE EXODUS FROM EGYPT TO THE PROMISED LAND —

There are characteristics or traits that can get you stuck in life. Some of these traits make you take one step forward and two steps backward. Murmuring and complaining are part of these traits.

The children of Israel murmured and complained every step of their journey. From the weather, to the food, to water, they murmured against Moses and God. A journey of eleven days took them forty years to arrive at the Promised Land. They were stuck for forty years, going around about the mountains of the wilderness. God is not holding anything back from you and me. There are traits that must get out of our lives, should we desire to move.

Every stylish way of murmuring against your pastor is limiting your progress. Stop complaining about your spouse. He or she is not your problem. Until you stop murmuring and complaining, you will be stuck. From your mother in-law to your boss at work, murmuring or complaining will not deliver your portion of the blessing. In fact, it can terminate your destiny.

> Neither let us tempt Christ, as some of them also tempted, and were destroyed of serpents. Neither murmur ye, as some of them also murmured, and were destroyed of the destroyer. (1 Corinthians 10:9–10)

Please be very careful about murmuring or complaining. Today, many Christians do not think of complaining as a wrongdoing or a sin, much less a deadly one. It cost many Israelites their lives. They complained about everything, and finally they griped about God. "And the children of Israel said unto them, Would to God we had died by the hand of the Lord in the land of Egypt, when we sat by the flesh pots, and when we did eat bread to the full; for ye have brought us forth into this wilderness, to kill this whole assembly with hunger" (Exodus 16:3).

When you hear Christians begin to say," I pay my tithe and I give good offering. I wonder why I am still in a financial mess," it is like saying "I have done my part, and God has failed to honor His part." Such talk or thinking will open the door for the destroyer to destroy your life. Thanks be to God, we live in the era of God's mercy and grace, where destruction is not drastic and instant as it was in the Old Testament. Every kind of complaint must be out of your system. Let us not take God for granted.

— TESTING GODS PATIENCE

Right from Egypt, the people started complaining. They said to Moses:

> Because there were no graves in Egypt, hast thou taken us away to die in the wilderness? Wherefore hast thou dealt thus with us, to carry us forth out of Egypt? Is not this the word that we did tell thee in Egypt, saying, Let us alone, that we may serve the Egyptians? For it had been better for us to serve the Egyptians, than that we should die in the wilderness. (Exodus 14:11–12)

They had forgotten the ten plagues that brought Egypt to her knees and secured their freedom. Instead of trusting that same God, their fears drove them to complaints. Even when God came through for them again and again, they still complained with every challenge they encountered.

> And the whole congregation of the children of Israel murmured against Moses and Aaron in the wilderness: And the children of Israel said unto them, Would to God we had died by the hand of the Lord in the land of Egypt, when we sat by the flesh pots, and when we did eat bread to the full; for ye have brought us forth

into this wilderness, to kill this whole assembly with hunger. (Exodus 16:2–3)

Some of them got burned up by fire. (Numbers 11:1-6). But that was not enough of a warning sign. Eventually, they started speaking harsh words against not only Moses but God.

And they journeyed from mount Hor by the way of the Red sea, to compass the land of Edom: and the soul of the people was much discouraged because of the way. And the people spake against God, and against Moses, Wherefore have ye brought us up out of Egypt to die in the wilderness? For there is no bread, neither is there any water; and our soul loatheth this light bread. (Numbers 21:4–5)

As this attitude continued, true to the word of God, of all that complained and murmured, not one of them entered the Promised Land. From twenty years and above, only Caleb and Joshua made it to the Promised Land. This pattern of murmuring continued among some of the people, even in the Promised Land.

Ye have said it is vain to serve God: and what profit is it that we have kept his ordinance, and that we have walked mournfully before the Lord of hosts? And now we call the proud happy; yea, they that work wickedness are set up; yea, they that tempt God are even delivered. (Malachi 3:14–15)

On July 3, 1993, I was down and frustrated. I was telling God how I have been faithful in paying my tithes, giving good offerings, going for evangelism, and doing a lot as a volunteer in the church. I complained a lot that day. I went ahead to justify my spirit of ingratitude. I was asking God, why should I give thanks, when nothing is going well for me? I was simply saying, "I'm faithful in doing my part, and God is not faithful in doing His part." How stupid and ignorant I was. All these complaints apparently had been inside of me all the while. The Fourth of July, which was the next day, was our thanksgiving service. As I stood in church during praise session, the Lord had mercy on me as I became aware of His presence all over me. I began to cry, and from deep within me, I heard these words, not loud but strong enough to cast a lasting effect on me! "I, the Lord, am a Faithful God." Since then, I have never doubted His faithfulness. Please, let us use great caution in our use of words. Please never, I say *never*, judge God. Even your thoughts are not hidden from Him. God cannot be deceived. He sees the deepest of thoughts. So be content with God and trust Him for the fullness of the blessing upon your life. Our Father is such a faithful and generous God, and He has your best interest at heart.

Therefore, let your faith be "abounding and over flowing in it with thanksgiving" (Colossians 2:7 AMPC). Instead of complaining, be thankful, knowing that God will neither leave nor forsake you. In the face of all unpleasantness, learn to be grateful. In all things, we are required to give thanks.

– AVOID STRIFE

With one stroke of a blow, the enemy can set you back for ten years or more, if he is able to deceive you into operating in strife.

What is strife? It is a lack of agreement or harmony between brothers and sisters, spouses or friends. When you allow a simple disagreement to turn into a bitter conflict, heated and often violent dissension, you are already in strife. Abraham knew the deadly effect of strife and took the necessary step to avoid it. As Abraham and Lot started prospering, their cattle and servants increased, and the land was not able to accommodate them.

> And there was a strife between the herdmen of
> Abram's cattle and the herdmen of Lot's cattle: and

the Canaanite and the Perizzite dwelled then in the land. And Abram said unto Lot, Let there be no strife, I pray thee, between me and thee, and between my herdmen and thy herdmen; for we be brethren. (Genesis 13:7–8)

Abraham will forever remain a perfect reference point of the blessing. He knew the dangerous consequence of strife and its effect on the blessing and immediately took steps to avoid it.

Is not the whole land before thee? separate thyself, I pray thee, from me: if thou wilt take the left hand, then I will go to the right; or if thou depart to the right hand, then I will go to the left Then Lot chose him all the plain of Jordan; and Lot journeyed east: and they separated themselves the one from the other. (Genesis 13:9,11)

Please understand that it is not the material possessions you have that make for the blessing. Rather, it is the Spirit of God working on your inside to manifest the blessing on the outside, so do not struggle or fight for things. True sons and daughters of the most high God know that material things are not the blessing. The source is much more important than the product of the source. Do everything in your power to avoid missing the source of the blessing by avoiding strife.

But foolish and unlearned questions avoid, knowing that they do gender strifes. And the servant of the Lord must not strive; but be gentle unto all men, apt to teach, patient. (2 Timothy 2:23–24)

In Christ Jesus, God has made all Christians priests, and as such, we are all servants of the Lord. Paul the apostle used a very strong word to instruct us. Speaking through the Spirit of God, he said we "must not be quarrelsome (fighting and contending)." Strife must be out of your life as a child of the most high God, as it brings you into captivity. To allow strife is to grant access to confusion (unrest, disharmony, rebellion) and all sorts of evil and vile practices in your life (James 3:16 AMPC). The blessing of the Lord cannot operate in such an atmosphere. Do everything to avoid strife.

There is no blessing being in bondage. If you have to forfeit your personal rights, let it go. Letting go of my right or opinion is far better than getting involved in strife. Remember, Abraham forfeited the best part of the land to Lot. For Abraham, nothing must affect the source of the blessing. He said to his nephew "if thou wilt take the left hand, then I will go to the right; or if thou depart to the right hand, then I will go to the left. And Lot lifted up his eyes, and beheld all the plain of Jordan, that it was well watered everywhere" (Genesis 13:9–10). Lot choose the best part, but that did not stop the blessing from increasing Abraham greatly. Abraham understood that the blessing was beyond the choice of Lot, or what we see or feel.

– FORGIVENESS

There is no doubt in my mind that God is ready to release the blessing upon His people. Expect great things to happen. This is your season, and your time is now! For you to activate the blessing of Abraham upon your life, you must walk in forgiveness. Unforgiveness causes a disconnection in the flow of your inheritance. You can choose to hold grudges and bitterness against your brother or sister, or you can decide to walk in forgiveness and love.

Forgiveness is not based on how we feel; instead it is based on our actions concerning what the word of God says. When bitter thoughts arise, do not nurse them. The mission of bitter thoughts is to hinder you and eventually destroy your life. So immediately when bitter thoughts arise, get rid of them. Attack them, as you would attack a venomous snake. It takes the love of God controlling you not to react, when others overstep their bounds. The mission of the enemy is to get you out of God's circle; he wants you bitter, angry, mad, and shouting violently to the dismay of everyone. Be wise. Nothing good ever comes out of quarreling. To walk in the blessing, by all means, "Do not be bitter or angry or mad. Never shout angrily or say things to hurt others. Never do anything evil" (Ephesians 4:31 NCV). Doing this will grieve the mighty One of Israel. Rather, Paul told us to, "Be kind and loving to each other, and forgive each other just as God forgave you in Christ" (Ephesians 4:32 NCV).

I have a principle I live by: have a lot of forgiveness in your heart, so you can give it out on credit whenever anyone offends you. Before they ask for forgiveness, you have forgiven them. It is better to forgive from your heart. Inability to forgive can hinder your walk with the Lord and stop your prayer life.

> And whenever you stand praying, if you have anything against anyone, forgive him and let it drop (leave it, let it go), in order that your Father Who is in heaven may also forgive you your own failings and shortcomings and let them drop. But if you do not forgive, neither will your Father in heaven forgive your failings and shortcomings. (Mark 11:25–26 AMPC)

Furthermore, it takes you away from the grace of God and breeds bitterness in you. Choose to forgive. The life of Joseph is one that exemplifies the uniqueness and power of forgiveness.

— THE STORY OF JOSEPH

Joseph had a very rough journey to the top. Think of it. It is like coming from the richest family on earth to becoming a slave boy in a strange land without father, mother, or any relative, and it all started due to the hatred the brothers had for him.

> Now Israel loved Joseph more than all his children, because he was the son of his old age: and he made him a coat of many colors. And when his brethren saw that their father loved him more than all his brethren, they hated him, and could not speak peaceably unto him. (Genesis 37:3–4)

Joseph loved his brothers, but they hated him. The brothers agreed to kill him but then decided to sell him as a slave.

> And it came to pass, when Joseph was come unto his brethren, that they stript Joseph out of his coat, his coat of many colours that was on him; Then there passed by Midianites merchantmen; and they drew and lifted up Joseph out of the pit, and sold Joseph to the Ishmeelites for twenty pieces of silver: and they brought Joseph into Egypt. (Genesis 37:23,28)

After Potiphar bought Joseph as his personal slave and brought him to his house, he made him the overseer of everything he had. The Lord blessed Potiphar's house with great favor and increase because of Joseph. However, from time to time the wife of Potiphar was making passes at Joseph, and one day she decided to force Joseph to commit adultery, but he refused and ran out of the room to save his destiny. Thus Joseph was accused of something he was innocent of. "And Joseph's master took him, and put him into the prison, a place where the king's prisoners were bound: and he was there in the prison" (Genesis 39:20). In the prison God was with Joseph, and he was promoted to be incharge of the prison. Then two inmates had a dream that troubled them. Joseph stepped in and interpreted their dreams, and both men were out of the prison. One was killed; the other gained his freedom and restoration as the butler of Pharaoh according to the interpretation of his dream. But he forgot Joseph for two whole years.

All these issues would have been enough for Joseph to be bitter and resentful toward these people. But he walked in forgiveness and love. One may say Joseph is a fool. "He should have given them a piece of his mind." No. That is not the way of the blessing. Joseph's decision to forgive enabled God to really bless him. There are things you need to overlook in order to walk in the higher ways of life. After two full years of freedom for Pharaoh's butler, the king of Egypt had a dream, and none could interpret it. Just about that time the butler remembered Joseph and informed Pharaoh. Joseph was brought in from the prison, and by the Spirit of God upon him, he was able to accurately interpret Pharaoh's dream. After the interpretation, the king said unto Joseph:

> Forasmuch as God hath shewed thee all this, there is none so discreet and wise as thou art: Thou shalt be over my house, and according unto thy word shall all my people be ruled: only in the throne will I be greater than thou. And Pharaoh said unto Joseph, See, I have set thee over all the land of Egypt. And Pharaoh took off his ring from his hand, and put it upon Joseph's hand, and arrayed him in vestures of fine linen, and put a gold chain about his neck; And he made him to ride in the second chariot which he had; and they cried before him, Bow the knee: and he made him ruler over all the land of Egypt. And Pharaoh said unto Joseph, I am Pharaoh, and without thee shall no man lift up his hand or foot in all the land of Egypt. (Genesis 41:39–44)

You will agree with me that the path of forgiveness and love is better than revenge. The life of Joseph is one of hope, faith, love, and forgiveness. With these virtues operating in your life, you are bound for the top. Who you walk with determines if you will get to your throne. Allow forgiveness to accompany you on your journey to greatness. I trust you will get to your throne as you walk with the Lord.

Another aspect of forgiveness is that you must learn to forgive yourself. When you are unable to forgive yourself for whatever reason, it is the same as refusing to forgive your neighbor, friend, or relative. God is not holding anything against you. The very day you accepted Christ Jesus as your Lord and Savior, your past sins were washed away. God is not the one reminding you of your past. Rather, He blots out and cancels your transgressions, for His own sake, and has decided not to remember your past mistakes (Isaiah 43:25 AMPC). No matter the nature of the sin, God is not holding it against you. Think of someone whom you love and treasure dearly. Right in your presence, he or she is using a knife, a sharp stone, or something else to inflict self-injury. Meanwhile, you have the skill and ability to take off the knife or sharp stone. Will you watch the one whom you love engage in an act of self-destruction, or will you intervene to save his or her life? I trust you will save the life of the one you love. In the same manner, God stepped in to save you when He sent Jesus to take your place. You need to forgive yourself "just as God forgave you in Christ" (Ephesians 4:32 NCV). In Christ Jesus, all our wrongdoings have been swallowed up. Be free from whatever prison you have put yourself in, in Jesus's name, Amen!

CHAPTER 7

CHANNELS OF
THE BLESSING

If ye be willing and obedient, ye shall eat the good of
the land. (Isaiah 1:19)

*Nothing will ever dominate your life unless it happens
daily.*

—Mike Murdock

On a daily basis we must learn to place value on the blessing of
Abraham. There is no greater asset you will ever have in life than
the blessing of the Lord. When you are able to lay hold on it, no one
will be able to deny you of its benefit. Abraham saw the blessing and
laid hold of it before he was blessed (Genesis 13:15). Everything you
will ever need to become great in this life is already packaged in
the blessing of Abraham. Remember, it is the blessing of Abraham,
which is the same as the blessing of the Lord, that makes one rich
(Proverbs 10:22). As a believer in Christ Jesus, you already have the
blessing of Abraham credited to your account. In this chapter, we are
looking at how to draw down from your account. Your willingness
and obedience to God's instructions will determine the extent of
your blessing.

However, preparation is a necessity to enjoying the blessing of
Abraham. Although you are entitled to the blessing of Abraham by
reason of your being in Christ Jesus, it will not manifest automatically.

You have a part to play: you have to brace up with preparation. You have to prepare yourself spiritually, mentally, and physically.

BRACE UP PREPARATION FOR PERFORMANCE

When you see a skyscraper, it stands out with its beauty and elegance. However, what the eyes cannot see are the tons upon tons of metals, pilings, concrete, and structural work buried underneath the skyscraper, which give the foundation support for it to tower high above. The same thing goes for a successful life with God. The depth of your preparation determines the height you will attain in life.

> So Jotham became mighty, because he prepared his ways before the Lord his God. (2 Chronicles 27:6)

Jotham succeeded in a big way due to his level of preparation. The blessing of the Lord did not come upon him by accident or coincidence or luck. It was a well-laid-out plan. Preparation is required for you to walk into the plan.

Preparation leads to greatness. When you are prepared, opportunity will show up. A lot of people are closed to opportunity because they are not prepared. When preparation meets with opportunity, greatness is inevitable. When you are prepared, you are quick to recognize opportunity and take advantage of it. I personally believe that every preparation should start with the word of God.

> And it shall come to pass, if thou shalt hearken diligently unto the voice of the Lord thy God, to observe and to do all his commandments which I command thee this day, that the Lord thy God will set thee on high above all nations of the earth: And all these blessings shall come on thee, and overtake thee, if thou shalt hearken unto the voice of the Lord thy God. (Deuteronomy 28:1–2)

The reason we spend time reading the Bible is so we can heed it and move in the direction God has predestined for us as His creations. This involves listening intently for the voice of the word, with a mind set to respond to the instructions forthwith. Preparation is of absolute necessity to follow God's instructions.

After the baptism of Jesus Christ, as part of His preparation for His earthly ministry, He was led by the Holy Spirit into the wilderness to be tempted by the devil. In response to one of the temptations, Jesus Christ made a very profound statement when He said:

> It has been written, Man shall not live and be upheld and sustained by bread alone, but by every word that comes forth from the mouth of God. (Matthew 4:4 AMPC)

The Bible from the book of Genesis to Revelation is God breathed. Reading the Bible with passion prepares you to live in the blessing of Abraham. Every word that comes from the mouth of God is designed to prepare you for your destiny and make you a champion in your world. When you spend time in the word, you are actually preparing and positioning yourself to walk with the Lord and be led by Him. Get yourself soaked in the Bible with understanding and purpose and you will begin to understand Proverbs 6:22: "When thou goest, it shall lead thee; when thou sleepest, it shall keep thee; and when thou awakest, it shall talk with thee." Good preparation will cause you to recognize the voice of the word, and whatever He tells you to do, just go ahead and do it.

Preparation brings out the best in you. Inside every child of God are treasures untold. Job was able to bounce back to life because the word had prepared him. When things were out of his control, only one thing was left with him: the word of God. He refused to let go of the word.

> But he knoweth the way that I take: when he hath tried me, I shall come forth as gold. My foot hath

held his steps, his way have I kept, and not declined. Neither have I gone back from the commandment of his lips; I have esteemed the words of his mouth more than my necessary food. (Job 23:10–12)

Job treasured God's instruction more than his necessary food. He was well prepared that his comeback brought him double restoration. The Lord's commandments are life and wealth to everyone who finds it. Brace up for relevant preparation.

There are various testimonies of believers all over the world who have immersed themselves into the word of God for days, weeks, and sometimes months searching for answers and directions. Jerry Savelle wrote in his book *In the Footsteps of a Prophet*: I studied the word just like it was my job. I knew how devoted I was to my job. So, I spent eight, ten, twelve, seventeen hours a day studying those tapes. I moved into that bedroom like it was my place of business and I spent not less than eight hours a day in the WORD. I came out at noon, had launch with the family, went back in there at 1:00, came out at 5:00, had dinner with the family, and then played with my daughters. When they went to bed, I went right back into that bedroom … at the end of those three months, I came out of that bedroom with the fire of God in my eyes, the word of God in my heart, the power of God in my hands and I was ready…

Today Jerry Savelle is a huge success story.

I love telling the success story of S. B. Fuller. He climbed to greatness from a very poor and humble background. He owns controlling interest in several companies. When asked the secret of his success, he said: "I knew what I wanted, but I didn't know how to get it. So I read the Bible and inspirational books for a purpose. I prayed for the knowledge to achieve my objectives. Three books played an important part in transforming my burning desire into reality. They were: (1) the Bible, (2) *Think and Grow Rich*, and (3) *The Secret of the Ages*. My greatest inspirations come from reading the Bible." When you are well prepared, you become well equipped to recognize divine opportunities.

In order to be able to control the wealth God has destined for you, you have to prepare your ways before the Lord your God.

These men all took responsibility to know, and it changed their entire lives, businesses, and ministries. If your life is not making progress, do not blame anyone. God is not to be blamed; neither the business nor ministry climate is responsible. Not even the devil is responsible. You are responsible. Give yourself to preparation before the Lord. Read the Bible and relevant books that have to do with your specific needs. Get acquainted with God, and stay with the word until every breath from you is fragranced with the word of life. Then you are set for the Blessed life, the glorious high throne that God has prepared for His people from the beginning.

— DO SOMETHING

> For the LORD your God has blessed you in all the work of your hand. (Deuteronomy 2:7 NKJV)

You have to do something to attract the Lord's blessing. The work of your hand is what God is committed to bless. For you to prosper in the blessing, you have to get a job, create a job, or invent something that the Lord will bless. If you are doing nothing, you should not expect the Lord to bless the work of your hand. God is committed to the person who is doing something. He will lead you to get a job or create one. To the righteous, God says in Isaiah 3:10 (NKJV), "That it shall be well with him: for they shall eat the fruit of their doings." To be alive and not do anything and expect the blessing of Abraham to prosper you is the greatest deceit of all time. In the first chapter of the book of Psalms, David talked about the man who is righteous and delights in the commandments of the Lord; in verse 3 he said that such a man will certainly be fruitful and he concluded by saying, "And whatever he does shall prosper." When it comes to Abraham's blessing, it is not what you are doing that makes for prosperity, but *the blessing* on what you are doing that makes all the difference.

Can you imagine trying to feed five thousand men, besides women and children, with five loaves bread and two fishes? You won't even think of it. But Jesus knew the power of the blessing. With the Lord's blessing on those five loaves and two fishes, it multiplied, fed everyone present with twelve baskets of fragments leftover! For anything to increase, you must have something for God to multiply. When you multiply nothing by a hundredfold return, the answer is still nothing!

Prayer, fasting, and confession alone will not do it. You need to get something to do. You might start with something small. That is all right, but by all means, do something. In God's kingdom, there is no room for laziness.

> He becomes poor who works with a slack and idle hand, but the hand of the diligent makes rich. (Proverbs 10:4 AMP)

"He becomes poor." He was not born poor; he became poor as a result of laziness and being idle with his hands. He might be confessing the word and praying but as long as he is not doing anything, he will certainly remain poor. Do not waste your life doing nothing. The scripture says, "He who sleeps in harvest is a son who causes shame" (Proverbs 10:5 AMPC). Do not sleep in your prime, for this is the time to work. Remember, the hand of the diligent results in riches.

Work is the will of God for you. It is your covenant right. In the beginning, Genesis 2:15 tells us that God required Adam to work by telling him to till the ground and keep it. A wise man once noted that, "God could have commanded the Angels or spoke a word to the garden to be tilled. But God did not do that, because He designed man to do it." This process that commits the God of Abraham in releasing a blessing for our labor has not changed, as we see it demonstrated in the earthly ministry of Jesus Christ. The Lord said, "My Father has been working until now, and I have been working" (John 5:17 NKJV). You have to be up and doing for the blessing to be made manifest in your life. Our heavenly Father is still working. Jesus worked while on this earth, and you just have to work. Remember, it is your God-given right to work. Instead of lazing about, the scripture says:

> Rather let him labor, working with his hands what is good, that he may have something. (Ephesians 4:28 NKJV)

For you to have "something" of financial reward, you have to labor, working with your own hands.

— BECOME A DILIGENT WORKER

You have to be diligent in all you set out to do because only the diligent hand will become rich. "Seest thou a man diligent in his business? he shall stand before kings; he shall not stand before mean men" (Proverbs 22:29). Being a person of diligence will cause you to stand out. Never be ashamed to start small. Joseph started his journey into the blessing of Abraham as a domestic staff; he was steadfast and diligent in the discharge of his duties. When you despise the days of little beginnings, you miss a great opportunity to be trusted by the Lord. "He who is faithful in a very little thing is faithful also in much, and he who is dishonest and unjust in a very little thing is dishonest and unjust also in much" (Luke 16:10 AMPC). When you are able to do well with little work, then much will be given to you. Commit yourself to be faithful and diligent in what you are doing. The hand of the diligent makes one rich. This is a divine principle that if you will decide to be diligent and faithful in the works of your hand irrespective of their size or nature, God will surely reward your labor.

Abraham, whom the Lord entered into covenant with to bless the entire world, was a cattle rearer. He also traded in silver and gold. He had something doing, and he was diligent about his business; therefore, God kept on increasing him to the extent that he was extremely rich! By now it should be clear to you that God will only bless the works of your hands.

The Lord shall command the blessing upon thee in thy storehouses, and in all that *thou settest thine hand unto*; and he shall bless thee in the land which the Lord thy God giveth thee. (Deuteronomy 28:8, emphasis mine)

You are next for the blessing to prosper. Get your hands on something, no matter how small, be diligent about it, and watch the God of Abraham take you from glory to glory.

— INVEST FOR THE FUTURE

The best way to remain poor, average, or in debt is to eat all your income or earnings, including your seed. Every month both seed and bread come as income. You must differentiate between your seed and your bread.

For as the rain cometh down, and the snow from heaven, and returneth not thither, but watereth the earth, and maketh it bring forth and bud, that it may give seed to the sower, and bread to the eater. (Isaiah 55:10)

Every successful farmer knows the importance of keeping the best part of the harvest for the next planting season. It is your seed that produces the next harvest; you cannot therefore afford to eat all your harvest. Consistently planting the best seed for the next harvest increases your harvest. We can see very clearly that Abraham's cattle kept increasing. The scripture records in Genesis 13:2 (AMP) that "Abram was extremely rich in livestock and in silver and in gold." We see the same trend in the life of Isaac:

And the man became great and gained more and more until he became very wealthy and distinguished; He owned flocks, herds, and a great supply of servants, and the Philistines envied him. (Genesis 26:13–14 AMPC)

To become great, you must apply this principle of setting aside. Consistency in so doing takes us to greater heights of wealth. Be like a wise and successful farmer by always separating the seed from the bread because the seed is meant to be replanted or invested. To ensure continuous increase in life, we must be conscious not to rob God. God must be paid first! It is called a tithe, which is 10 percent of our earnings. God demands it from us because that portion is God's, not yours. Moses instructed the people that "all the tithe of the land, whether of the seed of the land, or of the fruit of the tree, is the Lord's: it is holy unto the Lord" (Leviticus 27:30). After you have paid God, then you can pay yourself before any other obligation. Determine how much you will pay yourself, and this amount is your seed. The seed is not bread to be eaten. Rather, it is to be saved and invested for your future. Out of every income, a certain percentage (10 percent will be ideal to start with and should be increased with time) should be replanted for multiplication. This is how Jacob "increased and became exceedingly rich, and had many sheep and goats, and maidservants, menservants, camels, and donkeys" (Genesis 30:43 AMPC). This is still the plan of God for everyone today.

— SERVE WITH JOYFULNESS OF HEART —

Because thou servedst not the Lord thy God with joyfulness, and with gladness of heart, for the abundance of all things; Therefore shalt thou serve thine enemies which the Lord shall send against thee, in hunger, and in thirst, and in nakedness, and in want of all things: and he shall put a yoke of iron upon thy neck, until he have destroyed thee. (Deuteronomy 28:47–48)

God is looking for Christians who will serve Him with joy or great excitement. Whatever you are doing in the kingdom of God to advance the gospel is service. Get involved in your church, join a department, and serve. God has great plans for you in Christ Jesus. Serving God without delight and excitement brings one under the curse (self-inflicted curse). Serving God has become a burden and a duty to many believers in these times. Do not be part of that bunch. David the king was full of joy when the people said to him, "Let us go into the house of the Lord." You are to be delighted in serving the Lord, and your giving must be done joyfully. Show me a man who is excited in God and gives rejoicing, and I will show you a man who is destined for greatness. He will enjoy an overflowing portion of the blessing of Abraham. Yes, you might be facing a very challenging period right now, but God still demands that you consider Him faithful. Therefore, be excited in the most high God. A joyful lifestyle has been one of my greatest strengths in life and ministry. Knowing that God is faithful just keeps me going.

In the book of Malachi, the people used harsh words against God. They complained that serving God was not profitable and in (Malachi 3:15 AMPC), they went on to say that they consider, "The proud and arrogant to be happy and favored; evildoers are exalted and prosper; yes, and when they test God, they escape unpunished." Notice that these proud evildoers are happy serving the devil. Have you seen how fans, including believers, celebrate their football teams with excitement and joy during matches? But when it comes to the things of God, many are cold and rigid. You have to be deliberately passionate in your joyful service unto the Lord.

In the midst of those who complained, some were serving God and talking about His faithfulness with great joy. The scripture says,

> And the Lord hearkened, and heard it, and a book of remembrance was written before him for them that feared the Lord, and that thought upon his name. And they shall be mine, saith the Lord of hosts, in that day when I make up my jewels; and I will spare them, as a

man spareth his own son that serveth him. Then shall ye return, and discern between the righteous and the wicked, between him that serveth God and him that serveth him not. (Malachi 3:16–18)

The joy of the Lord generates inner strength that cannot be quantified. Do not allow anyone or anything to sap your joy. Go on and serve the Lord with great delight and excitement. Make a quality decision that you will not allow anyone or anything to take away or hinder your joy. To get offended or stay offended is a choice. Until you allow it, your joy cannot be taken away. Once your joy is taken, you will not be able to draw water out of the wells of salvation (Isaiah 12:3).

— ABRAHAMS GENEROSITY

Abraham lived a lifestyle of generosity. He loved giving to God and to man. When there was strife between Lot's herdsmen and his men and it became clear they needed to separate, he gave Lot the opportunity to choose first.

> "The whole land is there in front of you. If you go to the left, I will go to the right. If you go to the right, I will go to the left."… So Lot chose to move east and live in the Jordan Valley. In this way Abram and Lot separated. (Genesis 13:9, 11 NCV).

The portion Lot took was well watered, good for grazing. As the uncle and elderly one, Abraham should have chosen first, but he decided to be generous. Generosity does not take away from you; it only increases you more and more. In his generous lifestyle, he entertained angels without knowing who they were. He thought of them as strangers who just needed to refresh themselves for their journey ahead. Love for God was his motivating factor. Finally, he gave his one and only son whom he loved as a sacrifice in response to God's demand, and what was the result? "The Lord had blessed Abraham in all things" (Genesis 24:1). If you will not withhold any possession from the Lord, then there will be no limit to your greatness.

— THE SHUNAMMITE WOMAN

This woman's name was not mentioned in the scripture, but we will call her the Shunammite woman. This woman went out of her way with the consent of her husband to be generous to the man of God, Elisha. I believe Elisha was not the only person she was generous to, it was her lifestyle. Here is what happened as recorded in 2 Kings4:

> One day Elisha went on to Shunem, where a rich and influential woman lived, who insisted on his eating a meal. Afterward, whenever he passed by, he stopped there for a meal. And she said to her husband, Behold now, I perceive that this is a holy man of God who passes by continually. Let us make a small chamber on the housetop and put there for him a bed, a table, a chair, and a lamp. Then whenever he comes to us, he can go up the outside stairs and rest here. (2 Kings 4:8–10 AMPC)

She started by first offering Elisha a meal whenever he passed by, and then she decided that a little chamber for him to rest in would be great. She was not doing it because she wanted something from the man of God; it was her lifestyle. She loved to be good to people. To flourish in the blessing of Abraham, you need to learn to be good to people. The Shunammite woman was blessed according to the word of God (Matthew 10:41–42). She conceived and bore a son, which is a blessing money cannot buy. The son grew, got sick, and died. Her generosity spoke on her behalf, and the son was restored to life (2 Kings 4:18–44).

Read through the Bible, and you will notice men and women who were generous in their lifestyle. Your generosity takes you to a higher level—the lifestyle of Abraham.

— GIVING

Abraham succeeded in the blessing because he built his life upon the word of God. He fully obeyed God's instructions.

> It is written, Man shall not live by bread alone, but by every word that proceedeth out of the mouth of God. (Matthew 4:4)

What is the value of God's word to you, personally? Only the word of God can stand the test of time. Every time you obey His instructions, you are building on the Rock that cannot fail. David, the king of Israel, embraced God's word, and after more than three thousand years, his victory over Jerusalem is still being celebrated. Every word of God has the capacity to enable you to build lasting legacies.

Giving is an instruction from the mouth of God. It is time to start building to enlarge your financial destiny. "Take fast hold of instruction; let her not go: keep her; for she is thy life" (Proverbs 4:13). Every instruction from the Bible, when obeyed, gives life! Your giving connects you to the blessing of the Lord. When Abraham gave his tithe, Melchizedek blessed him. Isaac pronounced the blessing upon Jacob after receiving venison from him.

God Himself taught us the importance of giving. Before man was created, everything he would ever need was provided for and provided in abundance. There is no lack in the garden of Eden. The Lord has not stopped giving; He is still giving, because giving is part of the nature of God.

For God so loved the world, that he gave his only begotten Son, that whosoever believeth in him should not perish, but have everlasting life. (John 3:16)

Our Father in heaven doesn't just give but gives the best. Everyone who will increase and keep on increasing is always a great giver.

Giving is a proof that you have conquered greed.
—Mike Murdock

THE GIVING GRACE

I was studying a book titled *Super Abundant Prosperity* written by my father in the Lord, Dr. Sam Amaga. At about 6:40a.m. on March 15, 1997, the Lord spoke to me. Deep from my inside, I heard these words: "It is not yet time for eating. Rather, it is time for investing. It is the time to excel in giving grace. Therefore, exercise yourself in this grace, that you may excel in your time of harvest." This was the first time I was hearing these words *giving grace*. Later on, I saw it was in the scriptures, and I have been obedient to the heavenly instruction.

Paul was talking about the Macedonian church, using them to stir up the Corinthian Church. He said:

They have been tested by great troubles, and they are very poor. But they gave much because of their great joy. I can tell you that they gave as much as they were able and even more than they could afford. No one told them to do it. And they gave in a way we did not expect: They first gave themselves to the Lord and to us. This is what God wants. (2 Corinthians 8:2–3,5 NCV)

God wants you first and foremost. Your heart is much more important to the Almighty.

> You are rich in everything-in faith, in speaking, in knowledge, in truly wanting to help, and in the love you learned from us. In the same way, be strong also in *the grace of giving.* (2 Corinthians 8:7 NCV, emphasis mine)

The Corinthian church was the most gifted church as they were strong in the demonstration of the various gifts of the spirit. Although the gift of the word of wisdom, healing, and other gifts were flowing in the church, they were weak in the grace of giving. Paul had to ask the church to be strong in the giving grace that they may excel in the time of harvest. Jesus Christ became poor for your sake, that you might be rich (2 Corinthians 8:9). Jesus Christ is the one who brought us to partake in the blessings of Abraham. He became poor for our sake, and through His poverty, we became rich. Your background, your education, or your connections are irrelevant here, as God is set to make you a show piece. This same Christ Jesus said: "Give, and it shall be given unto you; good measure, pressed down, and shaken together, and running over, shall men give into your bosom. For with the same measure that ye mete withal it shall be measured to you again" (Luke 6:38). The quality of your giving will determine what you will receive.

> But this I say, He which soweth sparingly shall reap also sparingly; and he which soweth bountifully shall reap also bountifully. Every man according as he purposeth in his heart, so let him give; not grudgingly, or of necessity: for God loveth a cheerful giver. (2 Corinthians 9:6–7)

In the kingdom of God, what and how you give is important. Do not get carried away by your offering. From what is left after you have given, you will know a good offering. An adult-size elephant eats about 140kilograms of hay or straw in a day and produces about 100kilograms of manure within twenty-four hours. To eat like an elephant and release like a cow will definitely lead to destruction. Balance your outflow with your income. God is the one giving you the seed. Do not get too smart for the Lord. Learn not to consume all your income on yourself. Apart from giving your tithe and a good offering, be a source of blessing to someone who is financially in need. The Bible says there will always be the poor among us; minister to them with your resources, and do all your giving cheerfully. Why? God loves it when you are a cheerful giver.

When God's word penetrates your mind on giving, a revolution takes place. A force beyond the natural realm is released into your being, which makes for an exceptional harvest. This force is called *grace*. God's intention is to bring you into all-around sufficiency, where you are blessed beyond measure. The scripture says,

> God is able to make all grace (every favor and earthly blessing) come to you in abundance, so that you may always and under all circumstances and whatever the need be self-sufficient [possessing enough to require no aid or support and furnished in abundance for every good work and charitable donation]. (2 Corinthians 9:8 AMPC)

— DEVELOP A GENEROUS LIFESTYLE —

The Lord who created the heavens and the earth is a generous God. Look at everything He created. They are in abundance. Before He created Adam and Eve, He had created everything for them to enjoy. Everything needed was carefully provided for. Look at the vast expanse of land everywhere. The various mineral deposits are still being mined to date. Take water, for instance. He made sure there is no scarcity of water. Look at the world of trees and vegetation. The garden of Eden was generously furnished with the best of everything for Adam and Eve. All creation bears witness to the generosity of our God, and He in turn expect us to be generous.

There will always be people who will be in need of what you possess. Moses in Deuteronomy 15:10 (NIV) instructed the Israelites to "Give generously to them and do so without a grudging heart; then because of this the Lord your God will bless you in all your work and in everything you put your hand to." You need the blessing of Abraham to come upon the works of your hands.

CHAPTER 8

THE PRAYER ADVANTAGE

Abraham got up early in the morning to the place where he stood before the Lord. (Genesis 19:27)

And he spake a parable unto them to this end, that men ought always to pray, and not to faint. (Luke 18:1)

— DESPERATE FOR A BREATH

An effective and consistent prayer lifestyle is necessary to enjoy the blessing of Abraham. Prayer is vital to the working of the blessing of the Lord because it connects us to the power source. It is simply communion with God. Remember that Jesus Christ is the blessing. In prayer one is in touch with Him. The blessing of Abraham is of greatness, and God says to call upon Him and He will answer you and show you great and mighty things you know not (Jeremiah 33:3). In the place of prayer, we draw down our blessing. We have to be desperate for the presence of God.

As a little boy, say about nine years old or thereabouts, I went to the creek to swim. About that time, I was just learning to swim and was highly fascinated with the idea. Even though I didn't know much about swimming, at least I was floating. One day I decided to swim alone underneath a large anchored canoe used for transporting sand to the shore. The distance of the base probably might be about 1.5 meters. For me this was something I had been longing to achieve, and

I had seen others do it with ease. So on this day, I dived in to swim to the other side, and after a few seconds, I thought I was already there, so I raised my head up and heard a bang. It was my head hitting the bottom of the canoe. I became very desperate to get out from under the canoe. This was the longest time I had gone without breathing, and I was seriously in need of oxygen. So with all my strength left, I managed to get out on the other side.

— YOU NEED HIS PRESENCE

While I was underneath the canoe and gasping for breath, I would have done anything in exchange for oxygen. That is to let you know how eager and desperate I was to breathe. In the same way we should be desperate for the presence of God. Prayer is one of the ways we come into His presence. Prayer to the believer is what oxygen is to your lungs. Without a consistent prayer life, you will miss out a great deal on the blessing of Abraham. You must make prayer a vital aspect of your life, and then you won't be able to do without it. Remember what Jesus said, "He spake a parable unto them to this end, that men ought always to pray, and not to faint" (Luke 18:1). We just cannot afford to relent when it comes to prayer. It is something we must do to enjoy the Father's inheritance stored up for us.

— EXCUSES

As a pastor I hear Christians give flimsy excuses for their inability to pray. First, they claim to be too busy or not have enough time to pray. Now this is not very correct because we always create time for what we treasure, like eating, sleeping, studying, working, vacationing, family time, and many more. However, sooner or later you will be in a position where you need the divine help of God like I did, right in the water underneath the canoe, desperate for breath. The earlier you start a daily relationship with your heavenly Father, the faster your confidence will be established in the covenant of the blessing of Abraham. Second, some do not know what to say unto God. I was in that state some two decades ago. Within five to seven minutes after starting to pray, I would often run out of words in communicating with my Father, who is eager and longing to hear from me. God takes delight in hearing from us (Songs of Solomon 2:14).

Let me repeat it again for emphasis: without a consistent prayer life, you will miss out a great deal on the blessing of the Lord. Prayer must become a vital aspect of your life, and then you won't be able to do without it. You must create time to pray irrespective of other things that compete with your time. Abraham would always wake up early in the morning to pray (Genesis 19:27). Also, David was in the habit of seeking the Lord early (Psalm 63:1). In essence, spending time with God was given top priority. Once we connect with God first thing, wisdom and divine strength are released to deal with issues of life. Jesus never took for granted His relationship with God. As long as He was on earth, He depended on prayer to receive mercy and grace for His life and assignment. The scripture says, "And in the morning, rising up a great while before day, he went out, and departed into a solitary place, and there prayed" (Mark 1:35). Even when the multitudes sought after Him, it did not interfere with His prayer time. Jesus insisted that the disciples get in the boat and go on ahead to the other side while He dismissed the people to be alone and pray (Matthew 14:22 MSG). The word says, "With the crowd dispersed, he climbed the mountain so *he could be by himself and pray.* He stayed there alone, late into the night" (Matthew 14:22–23 MSG, emphasis mine). The King James Version says that Jesus sent the multitudes away in order to be by Himself to pray. To spend time with the heavenly Father, therefore, some things have to be sent away! People, projects, packages, television, social media, just name it—they need to be kept aside for the most important Person in life.

— RAISE AN ALTAR

Abraham, to whom the Lord swore that "in blessing I will bless you," was constantly in touch with the almighty God, as recorded in Genesis 12 and 13. He built an altar in every location wherever he resided. The altar was the place where he had regular times of meeting with God. As you read through the book of Genesis, you will discover that Isaac and Jacob did the same thing. They were constantly in communion with the almighty God. It is important for you to raise an altar unto God, a place of prayer, communion, or appointment with God. Before we proceed to study how and what to pray for, I want to share with you one of the secrets of a successful prayer life.

— MEDITATION

One of the reasons why so many believers are frustrated in their prayer life is unanswered prayers. On the other hand, you are filled with joy when your prayers are answered, and you are motivated to stay connected as you go into your closet to commune with your heavenly Father. Therefore, obtaining answers to your prayers is of utmost importance, and meditation on God's word is what guaranties results in your prayer adventure. All the covenant men and women in the Bible were people who spent time to excogitate the scriptures. Abraham, Isaac, Jacob, Joseph, Joshua, and numerous others invested ample time musing with the word. We can see from the scripture that God clearly instructed Joshua on the need for meditation.

> This book of the law shall not depart out of thy mouth; but thou shalt meditate therein day and night, that thou mayest observe to do according to all that is written therein: for then thou shalt make thy way prosperous, and then thou shalt have good success. Have not I commanded thee? Be strong and of a good

courage; be not afraid, neither be thou dismayed: for the Lord thy God is with thee whithersoever thou goest. (Joshua 1:8–9)

You have to look for a quiet place to think deeply on the word. For Isaac, he located a quiet place—one that suited his comfort and purpose. "Isaac went out to meditate in the field at the eventide: and he lifted up his eyes, and saw, and, behold, the camels were coming" (Genesis 24:63). You need a place that is convenient and easily accessible.

What Is meditation? According to the WordWeb dictionary, to meditate means; think deeply about a subject over a period of time; chew over, contemplate, excogitate, mull, mull over, muse, ponder, reflect, ruminate, speculate, think over … To meditate on the word is to think deeply on the promises of scripture as it relates to your desire. For me it means to personalize the promise; for example, the Bible says: "Himself took our infirmities, and bare our sicknesses" (Matthew 8:17) and "By whose stripes ye were healed" (1 Peter 2:24). When I meditate on these verses, I mutter, "Jesus Christ, Himself took my infirmities and bore my sicknesses, and with His stripes I am healed." As I speak these blessings over and over, I reflect on the work of the Messiah on the cross of Calvary, and I express my gratitude to God my Father, because He did not send an angel. Rather, He sent His only begotten Son to take my sicknesses and diseases away! You do not have to wait until you are sick to meditate on these scriptures. Meditating on the covenant promises regularly entrenches faith, thereby extinguishing and forcing out every doubt, unbelief, and fear from your life. This deliberate pondering, musing, and excogitating stirs the Holy Spirit to throw light onto the scripture, thereby illuminating your mind and showing you deep things about the promises of God, and as a result, your life is undeniably transformed. Oh what a rewarding and joyful communion with our heavenly Father!

— THE PRAYER PATTERN

The best way to know how and what to pray is to read the stories about Jesus in the gospels. No one ever prayed like Jesus did. He was prayer personified, and when His disciples saw Him pray, they were astonished. Afterward, they asked Him to teach them how to pray. So Jesus willingly did because He wanted them to be productive in their relationship with the heavenly Father.

> After this manner therefore pray ye: Our Father which art in heaven, Hallowed be thy name. Thy kingdom come. Thy will be done in earth, as it is in heaven. Give us this day our daily bread. And forgive us our debts, as we forgive our debtors. And lead us not into temptation, but deliver us from evil: For thine is the kingdom, and the power, and the glory, for ever. Amen. (Matthew 6:9–13)

This model of praying the Lord's Prayer was what delivered me from lack of what to say to my Father. From the above scripture and other numerous verses from the Holy Bible, we can break it into four categories, namely: worship, confession, petition and thanksgiving.

Worship: "Our Father which art in heaven, Hallowed be thy name." The word *hallow* means to honor as holy, it also means to bless: "Bless the Lord, O my soul: and all that is within me, bless his holy name. Bless the Lord, O my soul, and forget not all his benefits" (Psalm 103:1–2). You know that the name of the Lord is a strong tower, and as we worship His name, He spreads His wings of protection over us (Proverbs 18:10). Personally, I spend time to adore His redemptive names, like Jehovah—Mekaddishkem, Tsidkenu, Shalom, Rapha, Jireh, etc. These names are so revealing and powerful.

Confession: "Forgive us our debts, as we forgive our debtors." Honesty is very important in this part of the prayer. It requires you to reflect through the day, look deep into your soul and repent of all wrongdoings. Suppose you were extremely harsh in your words to your spouse or your coworker and the thought of it arose within you. Do not justify yourself but simply repent and ask God to forgive your actions. Remember, the scripture says, "If we confess our sins, he is faithful and just to forgive us our sins, and to cleanse us from all unrighteousness" (1 John 1:9). This gives you freedom to stretch deeper into God.

Petition: "Thy kingdom come. Thy will be done in earth, as it is in heaven. Give us this day our daily bread." The Lord demands that we invoke His kingdom over our lives on a daily basis, and by so doing, we will be enthroning His kingdom over every facet of our lives. In this regard, there is a dimension of forceful implementation of His kingdom as it is in heaven here on earth. This is actually the process of decreeing the establishment of His kingdom and will here on earth. This has to do with you being specific with the Lord in making your requests. Declare over your life, "Thy kingdom come. Thy will be done in my life." Pray His will over your life, your immediate family, your church, your relatives, your friends, your nation, and finally your personal needs. Remember that the will of God is the same as the word of God.

Thanksgiving: "For thine is the kingdom, and the power, and the glory, for ever." The Bible says it is a good thing to give thanks unto the Lord (Psalm 92:1). As you conclude your prayers, it is important to show gratitude unto the Lord as you thank Him for who He is and what He has already done. Thank Him because you have a relationship with Him through Jesus Christ and you can call Him Father! Thanking the Lord on a regular basis will give you an edge of victory in life. Thanksgiving puts you in the will of God (1 Thessalonians 5:18), and it is the password that grants you access into His presence (Psalm 100:4 MSG).

Since prayer is not the subject of this book, I will recommend you read *Could You Not Tarry with God for One Hour* by Larry Lea, *Too Busy Not to Pray* by Bill Hybels, *The Weapon of Prayer* by E. M. Bounds, and *The Circle Maker* by Mark Battererson.

— FOCUS ON THE GREATNESS OF GOD —————

As you pray the will of God, remember not to focus on your inability or inadequacies. Rather your focus should be on the greatness of God. This is one of the advantages Abraham had over the hopeless situation he was in. He decided to take his focus *away* from his shortcomings and redirected it on what God said, knowing that God Almighty is the God of all flesh. This is what happened as recorded in the Holy word.

> When everything was hopeless, Abraham believed anyway, deciding to live not on the basis of what he saw he couldn't do but on what God said he would do. And so he was made father of a multitude of peoples. God himself said to him, "You're going to have a big family, Abraham!" Abraham didn't focus on his own impotence and say, "It's hopeless. This hundred-year-old body could never father a child." Nor did he survey Sarah's decades of infertility and give up. He didn't tiptoe around God's promise asking cautiously skeptical questions. He plunged into the promise and came up strong, ready for God, sure that God would make good on what he had said. That's why it is said, "Abraham was declared fit before God by trusting God to set him right." But it's not just Abraham; it's also us! The same thing gets said about us when we embrace and believe the One who brought Jesus to life when the conditions were equally hopeless. The sacrificed Jesus made us fit for God, set us right with God. (Romans 4:18–25 MSG)

To enjoy the blessing of the Lord, you must have a consistent prayer lifestyle. This will make a great difference in your perspective in life. Do you know that what we call a barrier does not exist with God?

His ability knows no barricade, and prayer makes God's tremendous power available to overcome every mountain and get your needs met. Abraham prayed, David the king prayed, Jesus Christ prayed, Paul the apostle prayed; you just need to pray.

CHAPTER 9

RECEIVING IN THE BLESSING

> And I will make of thee a great nation, and I will
> bless thee, and make thy name great; and thou shalt
> be a blessing: And I will bless them that bless thee,
> and curse him that curseth thee: and in thee shall all
> families of the earth be blessed. (Genesis 12:2–3)

The Jews are a wonderful set of people who qualify to be called a blessed people. With families intact and businesses flourishing, they are the envy of nations. They are firmly in control of the things around them and are special because they believe in the blessing of Abraham. The Jews who do not believe in the blessing of Abraham are not stable. They cannot be compared to the ones who believe and trust in the God of their father, Abraham.

Remember, Jacob had twelve sons, and only one of them believed in the God of his grandfather. Joseph believed in the inheritance of his ancestry and was made the ruler and lord over the land of Egypt. At the same time Joseph was reigning in Egypt, his other brothers were looking for food to eat during the time of famine. It was the blessing that separated Joseph from the others. This same blessing has been extended to you and me.

> For the promise, that he should be the heir of the
> world, was not to Abraham, or to his seed, through
> the law, but through the righteousness of faith. For
> if they which are of the law be heirs, faith is made

void, and the promise made of none effect: Therefore it is of faith, that it might be by grace; to the end the promise might be sure to all the seed; not to that only which is of the law, but to that also which is of the faith of Abraham; who is the father of us all. (Romans 4:13–14,16)

Take note of, "to all the seed." To whom does the phrase to *all the seed* refer? Let's look at verse 16 from the Amplified Translation.

Therefore, inheriting the promise is the outcome of faith and depends entirely on faith, in order that it might be given as an act of grace (unmerited favor), to make it stable and valid and guaranteed to all his descendants—not only to the devotees and adherents of the Law, but also to those who share the faith of Abraham, who is thus the father of us all. (Romans 4:16 AMPC)

It is faith in God that makes the blessing stable and valid. It is guaranteed not only to the devotees and adherents of the law but also to those who share the faith of Abraham, the father of us all. Everyone who shares the faith of Abraham, in Jesus Christ, is a seed of God. When Paul the apostle talked of father of us all, he was referring to both Jews and non-Jews alike. In his writing to the Galatian Christians, he made it very clear to them, that because of Christ, they are now the offspring of Abraham: "Know ye therefore that they which are of faith, the same are the children of Abraham. So then they which be of faith are blessed with faithful Abraham. And if ye be Christ's, then are ye Abraham's seed, and heirs according to the promise." (Galatians 3:7,9,29).

Everyone who believes in the blessing of Abraham prospers in spirit, soul, and body. God has not changed; *Jesus is the same yesterday, today, and forever.* When we believe the blessing of Abraham, we are bound to prosper in the same manner.

— A PREPARED BLESSING JUST FOR YOU ——————

God is committed to perform His promise (oath), which is designed to bring you into a well-laid-out plan. You may not yet know you are walking in His plan, but when all is over, you will discover that truly, the good hand of God has been directing the events of your life!

> In Christ, there is no difference between Jew and Greek, slave and free person, male and female. You are all the same in Christ Jesus. You belong to Christ, so you are Abraham's descendants. You will inherit all of God's blessings because of the promise God made to Abraham. (Galatians 3:28–29 NCV)

As descendants of Abraham, God has willed His inheritance to all who belong to Christ. The scripture says, "You will inherit all of God's blessings." God did the same thing for Abraham. He was blessed in everything. When it comes to the kingdom of God, there is no luck or coincidence with the people of God. God knows when to bring the right people into your life. He can get you to be in the proper place with precise timing. Look at the sequence of events in Joseph's journey to becoming the prime minister of Egypt. Everything was planned and orchestrated by the heavenly host, and it was not a coincidence. Being a child of God who knows his or her right in Christ Jesus means you are into something extremely large. If Jesus tarries, Christians are going to make a huge difference to the entire world. This is the time, and now is the season. When this reality is able to get into your spirit, no force on earth will be able to resist you or stop you from becoming who God created you to be. Look at it: "You belong to Christ, so you are Abraham's descendants. You will inherit all of God's blessings because of the promise God made to Abraham" (Galatians 3:29 NCV). As far as the Almighty is concerned, He has spoken. Abraham believed it and possessed it. God said it; I believe it, and therefore, I am going all out for the blessing of the Lord.

You are to inherit all these blessings not because of you, but because of the promise God made to His friend Abraham, and God is committed to perform the oath (promise) He swore to Abraham. I must believe as Abraham believed. People of faith who believe usually declare where they stand with God's promises. A wise woman once said, "For you to receive the blessing of Abraham, you must have the faith of Abraham." God's blessing is waiting for you. God is most generous and extravagant in His provisions.

> For the Lord thy God bringeth thee into a good land, a land of brooks of water, of fountains and depths that spring out of valleys and hills; A land of wheat, and barley, and vines, and fig trees, and pomegranates; a land of oil olive, and honey; A land wherein thou shalt eat bread without scarceness, thou shalt not lack anything in it; a land whose stones are iron, and out of whose hills thou mayest dig brass. (Deuteronomy 8:7–9)

Everything is prepared for you to walk into it. One event will lead to the other and so on, which will bring you to your throne. The Israelites who obeyed God came into a prepared land. You are about to enter into your land. Remember, it is not because you are a very skilled, talented, beautiful, educated, or well-connected person. Thank God for these qualities. However, you are coming into this blessing for two reasons;

- You belong to Christ, so you are Abraham's descendants (Galatians 3:29 NCV).
- God made a promise to Abraham to bless you (Genesis 26:3).

God prepared everything before He brought in Adam and Eve into the garden. God has a garden prepared just for you, your spouse, your children, your job, your home, and so on. God is bringing you into your land, and the total package will be extremely delightsome.

— THE FAITH OF ABRAHAM

As a believer in Christ Jesus, you share the faith of Abraham. But what is the faith of Abraham? Understanding the faith of Abraham will help you understand how he received from God. Thirty days before Jesus ascended into heaven, He taught His disciples the secret.

After the resurrection of Jesus, before the disciples saw Jesus, they had seen the empty tomb, but He was not there. They only heard He was alive, from three of the followers of Jesus, including Mary Magdalene who told them that Jesus was alive. They doubted, since they had not seen Him physically. As they assembled together in the midst of their worry, doubt, and fear, Jesus appeared and spoke with them, giving instructions to them, and afterward vanished. Thomas was not with them when Jesus came, so they told him that they had seen the Master. Thomas said to them, "Except I shall see in his hands the print of the nails, and put my finger into the print of the nails, and thrust my hand into his side, I will not believe." Eight days after, Jesus came in with the doors shut. Boom! There He was in the midst of them. He went straight to Thomas and bid him to put his finger into His palm and to thrust into His side.

> Then He said to Thomas, "Reach your finger here, and look at My hands; and reach your hand here, and put it into My side. Do not be unbelieving, but believing." And Thomas answered and said to Him, "My Lord and my God!" Jesus said to him, "Thomas, because you have seen Me, you have believed. Blessed are those who have not seen and yet have believed."(John 20:27–29 NKJV)

Jesus used the occasion to teach them about the faith of Abraham. Blessed are they that have not seen and yet have believed. You have not seen God, you have not seen Jesus, but you believe they both exist. That is faith. Jesus said blessed are they who have not seen yet believed. You have to believe that God's word is true, in spite of the current situation facing you. Believe God can and will make the impossible turn around for your good.

– BELIEVING AS ABRAHAM DID

By now, you must have settled in your mind that God desires to bless you beyond measure. It is not because of what you have done or will do, but rather, He wants to bless you because He made a promise that He will bless you. It is all God's decision to make you a masterpiece. Actually, you can call it a divine setup. All you have to do is to believe and accept His blessing. That's exactly what Abraham did.

> That famous promise God gave Abraham—that he and his children would possess the earth—*was not given because of something Abraham did or would do*. It was based on God's decision to put everything together for him, which Abraham then entered when he believed. (Romans 4:13 MSG, emphasis mine)

All your skill, talent, and makeup are all part of God's divine setup, to bring you into His prepared blessing. While you appreciate God for your talents and all, remember, it is God's decision to bless you according to His promise. Isaac got the fulfillment of God's promise when he depended entirely on God and His ways of doing things. That is the only way everyone can be sure to get in on it. Take your eyes away from your circumstances, and focus your attention on God, who is able to make something out of nothing.

You have a famous promise from God—famous because it is the essence of the gospel of Christ and the root of Christianity. Abraham became famous because he laid hold of the promise of God. When the situation was hopeless, he dared to trust God to do what only God could do, and thereafter, the promise was fulfilled in his life. "The same thing gets said about us when we embrace and believe the One who brought Jesus to life when the conditions were equally hopeless" (Romans 4:24 MSG).

You have nothing to lose by believing the word of His promise. Rather you have all to gain. God wants to bless you, not because of your connections but because He made a promise to bless the descendants of Abraham. Your responsibility is to say, "Yes, I believe."

— DEVELOP YOUR FAITH AFTER GOD

> As it is written, I have made thee a father of many nations, before him whom he believed, even God, who quickeneth the dead, and calleth those things which be not as though they were. (Romans 4:17)

You need to understand that your words are as important as your life. Actually, Abraham learned this truth from God. He developed his faith after God. He discovered that when God was speaking with him, the Lord spoke of the future with much certainty, as though it already existed.

> We call Abraham "father" not because he got God's attention by living like a saint, but because God made something out of Abraham when he was a nobody. Isn't that what we've always read in Scripture, God saying to Abraham, "I set you up as father of many peoples"? Abraham was first named "father" and then became a father because he dared to trust God to do what only God could do: raise the dead to life, with a word make something out of nothing. When everything was hopeless, Abraham believed anyway, deciding to live not on the basis of what he saw he couldn't do but on what God said he would do. And so he was made father of a multitude of peoples. God himself said to him, "You're going to have a big family, Abraham!" "Abraham didn't

focus on his own impotence and say, "It's hopeless. This hundred-year-old body could never father a child." Nor did he survey Sarah's decades of infertility and give up. He didn't tiptoe around God's promise asking cautiously skeptical questions. He plunged into the promise and came up strong, ready for God, sure that God would make good on what he had said. That's why it is said, "Abraham was declared fit before God by trusting God to set him right." But it's not just Abraham; it's also us! The same thing gets said about us when we embrace and believe the One who brought Jesus to life when the conditions were equally hopeless. The sacrificed Jesus made us fit for God, set us right with God. (Romans 4:17–25 MSG)

I particularly like the phrase, "I set you up …" God knows how to set you up for the blessing to be actualized in your life! Notice, it was God who put everything together for Abraham. He set His friend up! He is about to do same for you! He is about to set you up for the most amazing blessing ever in your life!

With the word of God working in you, God can make something out of nothing, as you dare to trust Him. May be your situation has gone out of your control and there is little or no reason to stay alive. No matter how hopeless your situation, I encourage you to walk in the steps of this man who, when all things had become hopeless, believed anyway. He decided to *live not on the basis of what he saw he couldn't do but on what God said he would do, and so he was made father of a multitude of peoples.* God's word created all things; it can meet your need. For you to be ready for God, you must have a grip on the word. Abraham plunged into the promise and came up strong, ready for God, sure that God would make good what He had promised. You must realize that your words are as important as your faith. When he plunged into the word, he started speaking what he believed. He discovered that his words can have a direct impact on the blessing. Whatever you receive from the Lord will have direct link with your words. Speaking the word means that you do not say it casually once or twice but that you declare it confidently and consistently.

— BUILDING ON THE ROCK

Jesus gave us one of the greatest and surest ways to receive from the Father, who is reliable and consistent in word and action.

> Therefore whosoever heareth these sayings of mine, and doeth them, I will liken him unto a wise man, which built his house upon a rock: And the rain descended, and the floods came, and the winds blew, and beat upon that house; and it fell not: for it was founded upon a rock. And every one that heareth these sayings of mine, and doeth them not, shall be likened unto a foolish man, which built his house upon the sand: And the rain descended, and the floods came, and the winds blew, and beat upon that house; and it fell: and great was the fall of it. (Matthew 7:24–27)

Right in these verses is the foundation of your success or failure in life. Life has always been a choice. As I write this book, I live and work very close (say about four to five kilometers) to the Atlantic Ocean. A few years back, the waves of the ocean beat upon a long stretch of the seashore close to Victoria Island, and most of the lands, including part of the tarred road disappeared. The government stepped in and called in experts, and after a very tedious job, part of the beach was reclaimed, with heavy-duty rocks now placed between the Atlantic Ocean and land. This has prevented any form of erosion. Meanwhile, further down the beach, where there is no business activity as it is in Victoria Island (VI is a busy commercial center), a lot of houses in the community simply disappeared as the ocean waves carried them. The houses collapsed because their foundations were not deep or founded upon the rock.

Two persons were facing the same storm. After the storm, one stood out an overcomer while the other wailed all over the place. What is the difference? Imagine, two employees fired from their job on the same day. One laments, "Oh God, what will I do? I have nowhere to go. How can I get another job?" On and on he continued. The other employee got his letter, opened it, and read it. What he read was not pleasant, but this is what he said: "Praise God! Father, I don't know what has transpired for this to happen, but I know You have a better plan for me. I will trust You to take care of my family and provide me a better job." This man obviously is building on the rock and will not be disappointed. Sure enough, not long after that incident, he got a better-paying job.

Are you building your life on the "rock"? The rock is the word of the Lord. Begin to build your life on the eternal word of God. The storms of life come to everyone. You have to be prepared before it comes. Gloria Copeland once said, "The time of storm is not the time to build." During storms, you should be staying comfortably inside your fortified fortress. Can you imagine Noah trying to build the ark of safety during the flood?

When Isaac faced a very severe famine, it was the word (the Rock) that saw him through. Enjoying the blessing is a function of what is dominant in your spirit. Isaac had such a sweet fellowship with God's word.

> And there was a famine in the land, beside the first famine that was in the days of Abraham. And Isaac went unto Abimelech king of the Philistines unto Gerar. And the Lord appeared unto him, and said, Go not down into Egypt; dwell in the land which I shall tell thee of: Sojourn in this land, and I will be with thee, and will bless thee; for unto thee, and unto thy seed, I will give all these countries, and I will perform

the oath which I sware unto Abraham thy father. (Genesis 26:1–3)

So Isaac went ahead, stayed in the land, and planted in famine, a rare step of faith. Isaac, acting on the word from the highest authority, went and:

> sowed in that land, and received in the same year an hundredfold: and the Lord blessed him. And the man waxed great, and went forward, and grew until he became very great: For he had possession of flocks, and possession of herds, and great store of servants: and the Philistines envied him. (Genesis 26:12–14)

He became the envy of the entire nation. Your time for growth and expansion has come.

Without an iota of doubt, everything that will cause you to receive the blessing is in the word of God. Whatever you will ever need in life is in the Bible. You can build a fortress of love, great family, beautiful friendships, and unlimited financial resources from hearing and doing what the word says!

> This book of the law shall not depart out of thy mouth; but thou shalt meditate therein day and night, that thou mayest observe to do according to all that is written therein: for then thou shalt make thy way prosperous, and then thou shalt have good success. (Joshua 1:8)

Investing your time in reading and studying your Bible with the purpose of hearing and doing God's word is the greatest investment of your life.

— RELEASE THE ANGELS TO WORK ——————

Speaking God's word releases the angels to activate and deliver the blessing in your life. The angels are waiting on your words. We see this operation in the life of Daniel. He had been in prayer for three weeks talking to God. On the twenty-first day, an angel of God came to him and said:

> "Do not fear, Daniel, for from the first day that you set your heart to understand, and to humble yourself before your God, your words were heard; and I have come because of your words." (Daniel 10:12 NKJV)

Please note the point, "your words were heard; and I have come because of your words." The faith of Abraham was according to that which was spoken. Every time he called the name Sarah, he was actually speaking forth his desires: mother of multitudes. What is the promise of God to you? Abraham spoke based on God's word. Using your words to describe your situation makes the situation take root and stand firm or stable. Rather, use your words to change your situation. Learn to speak your expectation based on the promises of the word instead of speaking your current experience, knowing that your words are full of creative powers, either positive or negative. The scripture says right words are full of energy. Use your words to your advantage. I am not talking of chanting or repetition of words but speaking purposely based on the word of God for your progress. Listen to yourself speak. Do you like what you are hearing? If the answer is no, then you have to change the source of your information. You just cannot help but speak what is on your inside.

> O generation of vipers, how can ye, being evil, speak good things? for out of the abundance of the heart the mouth speaketh. A good man out of the good treasure of the heart bringeth forth good things: and an evil

man out of the evil treasure bringeth forth evil things.
(Matthew 12:34–35)

The mouth will speak out of the content of the heart. What controls your heart controls your destiny. What is in you controls what and how you talk. The angels do not carry out the negative words. No, they do not. The Lord has issued a command to the angels to wait on you. Referring to the angels, we are told they are ministering spirits. They are on standby to minister to every believer, who is speaking forth truth and the word of life. As it is documented in Hebrews 1:14, "Are they not all ministering spirits, sent forth to minister for them who shall be heirs of salvation?"

As you become a voice to the word of God, you give the angels work to do. "Bless the Lord, ye his angels, that excel in strength, that do his commandments, hearkening unto the voice of his word" (Psalm 103:20). You know, every child of God has an angel that ministers to him or her 24-7! They take every constructive word from your mouth and start working the blessing into your life.

> "Watch that you don't treat a single one of these childlike believers arrogantly. You realize, don't you, that their personal angels are constantly in touch with my Father in heaven?"(Matthew 18:10 MSG)

Did you see that? Your angel is constantly in touch with the almighty God, and in some cases, depending on your assignment, you could have more than one. Prophet Elisha had a host of angels watching and protecting him. The scripture says the mountain was full of horses and chariots of fire round about Elisha (2 Kings 15–17)! These angels were not visible to the ordinary eye. By faith Elisha knew they were there. Once the servant of Elisha was able to see them, he was no longer afraid. I hope your angel is not idle. If one is not enough, then more and more will be given to you, until you have a host of them like Elisha had. There is no scarcity of angels in heaven and on earth. Just for the record, one angel of the Lord slew

185,000 armies of the Assyrians (Isaiah 37:36). Psalm 91 is a passage you should read and meditate on.

> There shall no evil befall thee, neither shall any plague come nigh thy dwelling. For he shall give his angels charge over thee, to keep thee in all thy ways. They shall bear thee up in their hands, lest thou dash thy foot against a stone. (Psalm 91:10–12)

The key to enjoying these promises is, "I will say of the Lord, He is my refuge and my fortress: my God; in him will I trust" (Psalm 91:2). It is what you say that releases the angels to enforce a fortress about you and your family. Speaking words in line with the promises of God is as important to your enjoying the manifestation of the blessing, as breathing is to your lungs! Remember, Jesus said whatsoever you bind on earth will be bound in heaven and whatsoever you loose on earth will be loosed in heaven(Matthew 18:18). You have the mandate from Jesus.

Your words will keep you going and enjoying God, or they will get you stuck as did the Israelites in the wilderness. Speak only what you want to see. Speak of your dreams, of the greatness of your God, and of the help you keep receiving from the Lord. In other words, stop speaking your experience and start speaking your expectations.

One of the fathers of the gospel, Charles Capps, says, "God's word is His will to man. Man's words should be his will towards God. The angels know this, so they listen to your words, then they move busily about to cause it to come to pass or allow it to come to pass. The Spirit of God spoke to me and said, "If you speak sickness, disease, calamity, and bad things, the angels will surely not bring it to pass, nor cause it to come to pass. They will bow their heads, back off, and fold their hands, for you have bound them by the words of your mouth, and they cannot work for you. They will allow all the bad and evil to come to pass that you speak because your words are their warrant, and when you speak against their work, they cannot perform."

You were designed by the creator with the power of death and life in your tongue (Proverbs 18:21)!

Your life will never be better than the words from your mouth. What you are today is a reflection of what you have been speaking. If your angel is idle, it is a sign you have not been speaking right words, which is the word of God.

CHAPTER 10

GODS CIRCLE OF BLESSING!

> Where is the man who fears the Lord? God will teach him how to choose the best. He shall live within God's circle of blessing, and his children shall inherit the earth. Friendship with God is reserved for those who reverence him. With them alone he shares the secrets of his promises. (Psalm 25:12–14 TLB)

To live within God's circle of blessing is the desire of God for all His children. Our Father in heaven is pained when we live below our rights and privileges in Christ Jesus. God has made provision for everyone on earth to have more than enough. But unfortunately, only very few believers enter into this realm. However, the Lord wants you to live within His circle of blessing. There is a desire in every person to want more, and this is good as long as it is done with the right motive. Everyone wants to be great and famous. All these and much more are already packaged in the blessing of Abraham for you and me. Regrettably, the majority of Christians are pursuing these blessings without the Lord.

It seems that a lot of believers have forgotten that: "Except the Lord build the house, they labour in vain that build it: except the Lord keep the city, the watchman waketh but in vain" (Psalm 127:1). When you try to build without the Lord, you are working in vain, and therefore at the end of the job, you will be down to where you started from, and sometimes far below where you started from. You need the Lord to teach and guide you every step of the way as you walk with Him.

In the garden of Eden, Adam and Eve lived within God's circle of blessing. They were thoroughly and abundantly provided for. They lacked nothing, and they were never in need. The only desire or need they had was to meet with God Almighty and fellowship with Him on a daily basis. Truly, they were living within God's circle of blessing. God's circle of blessing, where every need was supernaturally provided for, was not designed for Adam and Eve alone but for every child of the most high God who will simply believe. This was His dream then, and His dream has not changed, for I am the Lord, I change not. Unfortunately, Adam and Eve disobeyed God and were driven out of God's circle of blessing. Since that time, humanity has been trying to get into God's presence without God. Any riches acquired outside God's principles or foundation will eventually collapse. It is like constructing the foundation of your house on the sand.

As long as there is rain, flood, and wind, it will surely crumble (Matthew 7:27).

— THE BABEL ENCOUNTER

Perhaps the story in Genesis will illustrate better what it means to build without God. As a child of God, you cannot afford to build a fortune without the Lord. The reason why so many have failed is because they are simply doing what these men did with the Tower of Babel. It will interest you to know that these men had the capacity to do anything they wanted. The Lord testifies to that when He said: "Now, these people are united, all speaking the same language. This is only the beginning of what they will do. They will be able to do anything they want" (Genesis 11:6 NCV). No matter your talent and resources, anything done outside of God will surely collapse; it is only a matter of time.

> And it came to pass, as they journeyed from the east, that they found a plain in the land of Shinar; and they dwelt there. And they said one to another, Go to, let us make brick, and burn them thoroughly. And they had brick for stone, and slime had they for mortar. And they said, Go to, let us build us a city and a tower, whose top may reach unto heaven; and let us make us a name, lest we be scattered abroad upon the face of the whole earth. (Genesis 11:2–4)

They knew God's plan, but they came up with a contrary plan. God's plan was for men and women to be spread abroad all over the earth. But they wanted to stay in the plain of Shinar and make for themselves a name, reputation, fame, and glory. They tried to do these things without the right foundation, so failure was inevitable. The Lord scattered them. You cannot go against God and succeed. There is no wisdom or counsel against the Lord that can prosper.

Meanwhile, God found a man called Abram (later called Abraham). When the Lord found Abraham, he was a nobody. The story of Abraham is like taking nothing and making something out of it, which only God can do.

> Now the Lord had said unto Abram, Get thee out of thy country, and from thy kindred, and from thy father's house, unto a land that I will shew thee: And I will make of thee a great nation, and I will bless thee, and make thy name great; and thou shalt be a blessing: And … in thee shall all families of the earth be blessed. (Genesis 12:1–3)

All the name, reputation, fame, and glory the men of Babel were looking for and much more were cheaply given to Abraham, all because he obeyed God's instruction. God is willing and ready to do much more for you. His faith brought him into the circle of blessing.

> By faith Abraham, when he was called to go out into a
> place which he should after receive for an inheritance,
> obeyed; and he went out, not knowing whither he
> went. For he looked for a city which hath foundations,
> whose builder and maker is God. (Hebrews 11:8,10)

Abraham never built without God. If you desire to live within God's circle of blessing, lay a foundation, and ensure that the builder and maker is God.

The Lord has shown us how to live within His circle of generosity. He has not left us without direction on how to enter into the supernatural supplies He has stored up for you and me. David having experienced the abundant provision of the Lord, exclaimed, "Oh how great is thy goodness, which thou hast laid up for them that fear thee; which thou hast wrought for them that trust in thee before the sons of men!" (Psalm 31:19). Everything you will ever have need of is already provided for! As children of the most high God, you can turn every dry land into a watered land! God has much in store than you will ever have need of, and you should expect great things to happen to you that may naturally not happen for others. You have something working for you. There is a weight of God's glory upon you! That glory is called favor. Please take note: it is not just favor but heavy favor that is upon you.

Dare to dream big, believe big, ask big, and expect big! The almighty God is on your side. Take advantage of your relationship with the Lord. His goodness toward you is great. You have to make up your mind and get acquainted with the word of God.

— RESPECT FOR GOD

Your reverence for God and His word will unlock the power resident in the written word of God. Walking in the fear of God has to be intentional. Make a deliberate decision to honor the Lord in your thinking, your words, and your actions. That is to say, holiness must become your lifestyle. It is a dimension of living a life that is pleasing to the Father by demonstrating willful obedience to the command of the word and the Spirit.

God, by His Holy Spirit, is always ready to lead us in choosing the best. You see, the Lord knows the way. He knows the end from the beginning. As long as you take God by His word and are walking in the light of the truth that you have, victory is sure to manifest. In some cases, things may not go the way you expect them, so do not give up. Stand your ground, because God knows what He is doing.

> Where is the man who fears the Lord? God will teach him how to choose the best. He shall live within God's circle of blessing, and his children shall inherit the earth. Friendship with God is reserved for those who reverence him. With them alone he shares the secrets of his promises. (Psalm 25:12–14 TLB)

When we walk with God in the light of His word, it is a demonstration of our love, respect, and reverence for the Lord. According to Bishop T. D. Jakes: Tithing is a matter of love. Obeying God's instruction on your tithe, which is ten per cent of all your income, is a demonstration of your love and respect for the Lord. The same thing goes when you forgive and show mercy to others and most importantly to yourself.

Position yourself to be led by the Holy Spirit. No matter how difficult the situation you are in right now, be rest assured that God knows the way out of it, because He is the way. Because you have chosen to honor and love the Lord, He will show you the way to live within God's circle of blessing.

The life of Joseph is a great example of living within God's circle of blessing. Once He passed the test of loving and honoring God, he never experienced lack. Joseph was a man who had great love and reverence for the Lord. In all his dealings, he decided to honor and respect the Lord. When he was betrayed by his brothers, he was not bitter toward them but was out to please God. Joseph's number-one goal was to honor the Lord. His reason for refusing to sleep with Potiphar's wife was as a result of his love and respect for God. Hear what Joseph said: "How then can I do this great wickedness, and sin against God?" Christians need to start considering God in their thinking, saying, and doing. This was Joseph's way of life. When God takes preeminence over your life, you will not want to do anything without His guidance and direction. The opportunity to love and honor the Lord comes to everyone on a daily basis as we make our choices or decisions in life. No matter your condition, choose to honor the Lord and you will experience that things will begin to change for the best. Every need of man has been covered by the promises of God. Therefore, do not go hunting for these blessings without the Lord! Stick with Him, and He will show *you how to choose the best.*

> Where is the man who fears the Lord? God will teach him how to choose the best. He shall live within God's circle of blessing, and his children shall inherit the earth. (Psalm 25:12–13 TLB)

CHAPTER 11

THE ULTIMATE BLESSING

> The blessing of the supreme God, Creator of heaven and earth, be upon you … and blessed be God, who has delivered your enemies over to you. (Genesis 14:19 TLB)

God Himself gave the blessing to Abraham, and it became the turning point in his life. He was blessed in every area one can imagine. He was extremely wealthy, strong, and healthy. He saw his children's children. Everyone who stood against him was defeated, including the four nations that made war with him: Bera king of Sodom, Birsha king of Gomorrah, Shinab king of Admah, Shemeber king of Zeboiim, and the king of Bela (that is, Zoar). He was a successful man by all standards.

> And Abraham was old, and well stricken in age: and the Lord had blessed Abraham in all things. (Genesis 24:1)

The Lord had blessed him in all things to the extent that he had the desire for nothing else but God. Yet in all these blessings, he did not get the full measure or the ultimate blessing. He had the promise, but he did not taste of the fullness of the blessing until the birth, death, and resurrection of Jesus Christ, born in Bethlehem, Son of the Living God.

> Jesus, when he had cried again with a loud voice, yielded up the ghost. And, behold, the veil of the temple was rent in twain from the top to the bottom; and the earth did quake, and the rocks rent; And the graves were opened; and many bodies of the saints which slept arose, And came out of the graves after his resurrection, and went into the holy city, and appeared unto many. (Matthew 27:50–53)

After the resurrection, many bodies of the saints that slept arose and were out of the graves. At this moment Abraham and other saints participated in the fullness of the gospel. For you and me, our case is different. Why? We are children born in due season. We are born again into the blessing of Abraham ratified in Christ Jesus. As believers, we have access to the fullness of the blessing, which is like the crown of the blessing of the Lord. The apostle Paul said in Romans 15:29, "When I come unto you, I shall come in the fullness of the blessing of the gospel of Christ." The Message Translation renders the word "fullness of the blessing" as "extravagant blessings." Get ready for the extravagant blessing of Christ, or as I like to refer to it, the ultimate blessing!

– CONNECTING AND ACTIVATING

How do we get the fullness of the blessing? Now, remember that though you are entitled to the blessing of Abraham, the blessing will not work automatically because you are a believer in Jesus Christ. You have to believe in the blessing and that God is able to perform it in your life. Abraham believed. So did Isaac and Jacob, and they enjoyed the blessing. According to Genesis 30:43, from ground zero, "The man increased and became exceedingly rich, and had many sheep and goats, and maidservants, menservants, camels, and donkeys." He was tremendously blessed.

Now, Jacob had twelve sons, all of whom were entitled to the blessing of Abraham. God had promised, "I will establish My covenant between Me and you and your descendants after you in their generations, for an everlasting covenant, to be God to you and your descendants after you" (Genesis 17:7 NKJV).

Unfortunately, only Joseph took advantage of the blessing. He believed it, and the blessing of the Lord worked for him. Though the blessing is yours in Christ Jesus, it does not work automatically. It has to be triggered by the carrier. The other eleven sons of Jacob did not reckon with their father's blessing. Probably due to ignorance, they did not follow the path of the blessing. They all had equal rights to the blessing. They did not believe in it and thus suffered the consequence of the famine that was upon the face of the earth.

THE LOVE OF GOD

The love factor activates the ultimate blessing because the love of *God* is the regulator of the flow of the blessing of Abraham. Love is what makes all the difference when it touches the kingdom of God. For Abraham to enter into the fullness of the blessing of the gospel, God had to release His only begotten Son, based on His love for humanity.

> For God so loved the world, that he gave his only
> begotten Son, that whosoever believeth in him should
> not perish, but have everlasting life. (John 3:16)

God first of all demonstrated His love for the human race by sacrificing His only begotten Son. It is with the same love that God has harvested millions and millions of children into His kingdom. This same love of God gives us access to the ultimate blessing. With love in your heart, the fullness of the blessing will be yours. Walking in the love of God is the *best* thing that will ever happen in your life. This very love of God therefore activates the blessing in your life.

In the book of 1 Corinthians 12, Paul spoke of different kinds of gifts, all designed to help us live a better life. But in the last verse, he spoke of a far greater or better gift, and he pointed us to how and the way to get this gift.

> But earnestly desire and zealously cultivate the greatest and best gifts and graces (the higher gifts and the choicest graces). And yet I will show you a still more excellent way one that is better by far and the highest of them all—love. (1 Corinthians 12:31 AMPC)

Nothing is as grand, pure, and powerful as the love of God. It gives you access to the ultimate blessing of the Lord.

So what is the love of God? This love is not the same as human love. Neither is it a natural love. It is the God kind of love, and it is born by the Spirit of God. Every child of God has this love on the inside.

> For God's love has been poured out in our hearts through the Holy Spirit Who has been given to us. (Romans 5:5 AMPC)

This love of God is already in your heart. If you are not using it, it is because you have locked it up or deliberately ignored it. The best definition of love that I know of is found in the letters of the apostle Paul to the Corinthians.

> Love endures long and is patient and kind; love never is envious nor boils over with jealousy, is not boastful or vainglorious, does not display itself haughtily. It is not conceited (arrogant and inflated with pride); it is not rude (unmannerly) and does not act unbecomingly. Love (God's love in us) does not insist on its own rights or its own way, for it is not self-seeking; it is not touchy or fretful or resentful; it takes no account of the evil done to it it pays no attention to a suffered wrong. It does not rejoice at injustice and unrighteousness, but

rejoices when right and truth prevail. Love bears up under anything and everything that comes, is ever ready to believe the best of every person, its hopes are fadeless under all circumstances, and it endures everything without weakening. Love never fails never fades out or becomes obsolete or comes to an end … And so faith, hope, love abide faith … these three; but the greatest of these is love. (1 Corinthians 13:4–8,13 AMPC)

– WHAT LOVE IS NOT

It is not *arrogant.*
It is not *inflated with pride.*
It does not behave *unmannerly.*
It does not act *unbecomingly.*
It does not *insist* on its *own.*
It does not *seek self.*
It is not *touchy, fretful,* or *resentful.*
It does not take *record of evil done to it.*
It pays no *attention* to a *suffered wrong.*
It does not *rejoice* at *injustice* and *unrighteousness.*

– WHAT LOVE IS

It *endures long.*
It is *patient.*
It is *kind.*
It *rejoices* when *right* and *truth prevail.*
It has *capacity* to *bear all things.*
It is ever ready to *believe* the *best of everyone.*
Its *hopes* are *fadeless* under all *circumstances.*
Love *endures everything without weakening.*

Love never fails.

— LOVE IS THE GREATEST

This love depends on the word and the Spirit of God to grow and mature. It does not rely on feelings. As a child of the most high God, you have been privileged to have the love of God dwelling inside of you. "For God's love has been poured out in our hearts through the Holy Spirit Who has been given to us" (Romans 5:5). Knowing that God's love is residing in us is the best thing that ever happened to you as a Christian. The reason most Christians do not achieve much is that they are not depending on the love of God, or ignorantly, they have locked away the love in their hearts. You have to deliberately start using the love of God. The more you use it, the more it increases and the better you become. Set the love of God in your heart free. Do not be afraid of those who will take advantage of you. The more you use it, the better things will begin to locate you. It is a law that goes beyond human thinking.

— THE MISSION OF LOVE

The love of God operating in our lives makes it easier to want to obey God. Obedience is very crucial in manifesting the blessing of the Lord, and because we love Him, we desire to obey Him. In fact, obedience is evidence that we love the God of Abraham, who is the *power* behind a blessed life.

> The person who has My commands and keeps them is the one who really loves Me; and whoever really loves Me will be loved by My Father, and I too will love him and will show (reveal, manifest) Myself to him. I will let Myself be clearly seen by him and make Myself real to him. Judas, not Iscariot, asked Him, Lord,

how is it that You will reveal Yourself make Yourself real to us and not to the world? Jesus answered, if a person really loves Me, he will keep My word obey My teaching; and My Father will love him, and We will come to him and make Our home (abode, special dwelling place) with him. Anyone who does not really love Me does not observe and obey My teaching. And the teaching which you hear and heed is not Mine, but comes from the Father Who sent Me. (John 14:21–24 AMPC)

Obeying God's word out of a pure heart due to love attracts His presence to be with you. Jesus said, He, the Father, will come to us and make our home (abode, special dwelling place) with us. Whenever you see the phrase "and the Lord was with him" success always follows. "And the Lord was with Joseph, and he was a prosperous man; and he was in the house of his master the Egyptian. And his master saw that the Lord was with him, and that the Lord made all that he did to prosper in his hand" (Genesis 39:2–3). As you take steps of obedience, the Lord will show up in your life, and your circumstances will never be the same. Remember, faith is taking God at His word. He said if you obey Him, He will reveal Himself to you and make His home with you.

– AFFECTION FOR GOD AND HIS KINGDOM

Affection is an expression of your love, demonstrating a positive feeling of liking toward God and His kingdom. When the rich young ruler came to Jesus and asked, "Which is the greatest commandment of the law?" this is what Jesus said:

You shall love the Lord your God with all your heart and with all your soul and with all your mind (intellect). This is the great (most important, principal) and first commandment. And a second is like it: You shall love your neighbor as you do yourself. These two commandments sum up and upon them depend all the Law and the Prophets. (Matthew 22:37–40 AMPC)

This is the kind of love that King Solomon had for the Lord. He loved God with everything in him. Begin to demonstrate your love for God.

And Solomon loved the Lord. (1 Kings 3:3)

The affection he had for God made him offer unto God one thousand burnt offerings. Your affection for God is what determines the flow of the blessing of the Lord into your life. One of the best ways to express your love is by giving. God the Father did just that by giving the most precious treasure for the freedom and good of the human race. That is exactly what God did for humanity, and you cannot love without demonstrating it.

For God so loved the world, that he gave his only begotten Son, that whosoever believeth in him should not perish, but have everlasting life. (John 3:16)

God's love for the human race compelled Him to offer His only begotten Son. He did not just pray or fast; He gave. Love will always move us to give and give, especially things we cherish. When your affection is toward God, you do not take offense when your needs are not met immediately. No matter your need, never allow yourself to get offended at anyone and especially at God. John the Baptist made that huge mistake, and it cost him his life. It is unfortunate the way John the Baptist died, but it ought not to be. For indeed, he was a great prophet. Even Herod the king was afraid of "John, knowing that he was a just man and an holy" (Mark 6:20). Speaking about the greatness of His forerunner, Jesus said, "Among them that are born of women there hath not risen a greater than John the Baptist"

(Matthew 11:11). According to the Holy Bible, of all men born from the time of Eve to the time Jesus came, John the Baptist was greater and mightier than all. Yet he died like a mere man. Why, at that time of his life, he had a need (we all have need for one thing or the other) for freedom. He was in prison, and while there he heard all the great and mighty works Jesus was doing and decided to send two of his disciples with a question to Jesus.

> Now when John had heard in the prison the works of Christ, he sent two of his disciples, And said unto him, Art thou he that should come, or do we look for another? (Matthew 11:2–3)

Perhaps John was expecting Jesus as the Messiah to come and deliver him out of the prison. For John to have doubted if Jesus is the true Messiah was a serious offense because he had seen the Spirit of God descending on Jesus at his baptism, heard a voice from heaven declaring Him to be the Son of God, often pointed Him out to others, and had borne frequent testimonies that He was the Lamb of God and Bridegroom of the Church. But faced with difficulty, he expressed doubt as to the identity of Jesus Christ. In answering the question of John the Baptist, Jesus concluded with a statement that is relevant and profitable to everyone: "Blessed is he, whosoever shall not be offended in me" (Matthew 11:6). Absolutely nothing is enough to make one take offense with God. With all the trials and challenges facing you right now, God is working to bring you out of it all. Let nothing put a division between you and your heavenly Father.

Paul asked a question: what shall separate us from the love of God? It was this same love that Abraham and David had for the Lord, which gave them a unique place with God through all eternity. Their love for God was unquestionable. The opening statement of the book of Matthew is attributed to these two men, whose love for God was undeniable.

> The book of the generation of Jesus Christ, the son of David, the son of Abraham. And Jesse begat David the

king; and David the king begat Solomon of her that
had been the wife of Urias. (Matthew 1:1, 6)

Note that among all the kings of Israel, only David was referred
to and documented as a king in the gospel according to Matthew. No
statement in the Bible is a mistake. The things you think, say, and
do tell a lot about your love for God. David demonstrated his love
for God by living a matching lifestyle. You are capable of loving the
Lord. Remember that God's love has been poured out in our hearts
through the Holy Spirit who has been given to us. Abraham made an
eternal impression in the heart of God when he obeyed and sacrificed
his only son, Isaac, whom he loved. The response of the Lord was so
pleasant, and the same response is what the Lord is going to bestow
on you upon your demonstration of His love.

> And the angel of the Lord called unto Abraham out
> of heaven the second time, And said, By myself have I
> sworn, saith the Lord, for because thou hast done this
> thing, and hast not withheld thy son, thine only son:
> That in blessing I will bless thee, and in multiplying I
> will multiply thy seed as the stars of the heaven, and
> as the sand which is upon the sea shore; and thy seed
> shall possess the gate of his enemies; And in thy seed
> shall all the nations of the earth be blessed; because
> thou hast obeyed my voice. (Genesis 22:15–18)

It takes love to go this length with the Lord. No gift coming from
you can make God richer. Rather, when it comes from you to the Lord
with love, it makes you richer from thirty to a thousand times more.
King David thus also demonstrated his affection for the kingdom
of God.

> Moreover, because I have set my affection to the house
> of my God, I have of mine own proper good, of gold
> and silver, which I have given to the house of my God,

over and above all that I have prepared for the holy house. (1 Chronicles 29:3)

This gift of love was from King David's personal treasury. It was not from the state account. This came out of his family treasure. Solomon had noticed his father was a fervent lover of God as well as a giver and chose to walk in the statutes of his father David, as he gave to the Lord a thousand burnt offerings, having been inspired by him.

– GIVE ALL OF YOURSELF TO THE LORD

My son, give me thine heart, and let thine eyes observe my ways. (Proverbs 23:26)

The ability to give yourself unreservedly to the Lord places you in the ultimate blessing. At this stage, as you learn to walk, listen for His instructions, and obey completely, you will not need to ask God for anything. Before you think or ask for it, the Lord will make advance provision. Is your heart in the blessing or in God? Those who seek after material things miss God. But those who seek after God automatically attract the blessing. Esau was much more interested in the physical than he was interested in God. Our focus must be defined as we seek God above material things. Gehazi pursued the material things and ended with leprosy.

The Macedonian church first of all gave their lives in totality to God before gifts. Is your heart with the Lord? Until your heart is with God, you will withhold things from Him. Abraham was completely surrendered to God; spirit, soul, and body, he was in God, and the Lord was with him. It was thus easy for Abraham to lay down the most precious treasure of his life—the only son whom he loved—in response to the sacrificial demand from God. Do you want to enjoy extravagant blessings from the God of heaven and earth? If your answer is yes, then give Him your heart. Once you give Him your heart, God becomes everything to you. What His word says is final to you. This is what it means to live a single and focused lifestyle. God alone is everything, and nothing should compete with Him.

> No man can serve two masters: for either he will hate the one, and love the other; or else he will hold to the one, and despise the other. Ye cannot serve God and mammon. Therefore I say unto you, Take no thought for your life, what ye shall eat, or what ye shall drink; nor yet for your body, what ye shall put on. Is not the life more than meat, and the body than raiment? Behold the fowls of the air: for they sow not, neither do they reap, nor gather into barns; yet your heavenly Father feedeth them. Are ye not much better than they? Which of you by taking thought can add one cubit unto his stature? And why take ye thought for raiment? Consider the lilies of the field, how they grow; they toil not, neither do they spin: And yet I say unto you, That even Solomon in all his glory was not arrayed like one of these. Wherefore, if God so clothe the grass of the field, which today is, and tomorrow is cast into the oven, shall he not much more clothe you, O ye of little faith? Therefore take no thought, saying, what shall we eat? or, what shall we drink? or, Wherewithal shall we be clothed? (For after all these things do the Gentiles seek:) for your heavenly Father knoweth that ye have need of all these things. But seek ye first the kingdom of God, and his righteousness; and all these things shall be added unto you. (Matthew 6:24–33)

The passage started by telling us that we cannot have two masters. Your heart cannot be focused on God and be focused on material things at the same time. "Take no thought, saying, what shall we," means do not worry over material things by way of thoughts or by words. We are instructed to be anxious for nothing. Anxiety is a sign your faith is about to drift or you no longer trust God. We do not need to get all worked up in the flesh, staying up at night worrying about material things. God our Father knows we have need for all these things. When you put God first, every other thing will follow. "But seek ye first the kingdom of God, and his righteousness" (Matthew 6:33). Give the Lord His place of honor, love, and kingship. Until you secure His presence, nothing is secure. Let every other thing wait. You need God. Fall in love with Him afresh, and give Him your heart!

The love of Christ in you enables you to put God first in all you do. Everyone who relied on this kind of love never failed in life. As you begin the practice of this love, it will be clear to you that "Christ's love is greater than anyone can ever know, but I pray that you will be able to know that love. Then you can be filled with the fullness of God. With God's power working in us, God can do much, much more than anything we can ask or imagine" (Ephesians 3:19–20 NCV). Thanks be to God that this love is already in every child of God.

The love of Christ is the ultimate blessing. As you keep on loving in line with the word of God, you will discover a stream of life flowing in and out of your being.

– PRAYER FOR SALVATION

Do you want to make Jesus the Lord of your life? Then pray with me: Dear God in heaven, I come to You in the name of Jesus to receive salvation and eternal life. I believe that Jesus is Your Son. I believe that He died on the cross for my sins, and that You raised Him from the dead. I receive Jesus now into my heart and make Him the Lord of my life. Jesus, come into my heart. I welcome You as my Lord and Savior. Father, I believe in my heart and confess with my mouth that I am saved and born again. According to Your word, I am now Your child. Thank You, Father. Amen.

Now you are born again. Start reading the Bible, and locate a church that boldly preaches God's word and practices it. Join a church family who will love and care for you as you love and care for them.

CPSIA information can be obtained
at www.ICGtesting.com
Printed in the USA
FFHW020609010619
52767790-58304FF

9 781973 615965